A Matter of Greed

A Matter of Greed

Arindam Mukherjee

The Institute for Economic Democracy

Institute for Economic Democracy
PO Box 309, Appomattox VA 24522, USA.

Printed in the United States of America
10 9 8 7 6 5 4 3 2 1

Library of Congress Cataloging-in-Publication Data

Mukherjee, Arindam.
    A matter of greed / Arindam Mukherjee, author. – 1st Edition.
        pages cm
    Includes bibliographical references and index.
    ISBN 978-1-933567-40-2 (case laminate bound : alk. paper) – ISBN 978-
1-933567-41-9 (perfect bound : alk. paper) – ISBN (invalid) 978-1-933567-42-
6 (epub) 1. Geopolitics–History. 2. United States–Foreign relations. 3. International relations–History. 4. Radicalism–Religious aspects–Islam. 5. Petroleum
industry and trade–Political aspects. I. Title.
    JC319.M85 2012
    327.1'110973–dc23

                        2012036075

Contents

Acknowledgments

For a corporate servant like me who hardly gets to travel to different locations other than for work, depending on a lot of books written by special people to build and enhance my comprehension of the world—irrespective of whether I write or just keep thinking, has become a way of life. The tremendous amount of constructive intelligence found within such books also probably augurs the end of the Old World Numbness, and when that eventually happens we shall remain eternally grateful to these writers, bloggers, journalists, observers, and researchers.

Heartfelt thanks to Professor Noam Chomsky—I still do not know what made you engage yourself to chat up with an unknown like me through mails for more than a year now; my friends envy me for that and I praise my luck secretly. Your blessings and your crucial inputs through personal notes, excerpts of speeches, suggested books, and kindly shared links, have bolstered my research, and made this book possible.

Salute to Pepe Escobar—the King of the Mavericks. Your book *Globalistan* got me thinking, your explanation on the works of Zygmunt Bauman or Emmanuel Wallerstein introduced me to a whole new world, and you have a role so fundamental to my point of view that it surprises me every day.

Thanks to Dr J.W. Smith of The Institute for Economic Democracy, for providing blanket approval to use his research materials, for sharing an unpublished manuscript from his treasure chest, for mentoring the birth of a brilliant new idea especially while composing the final chapter, and for those long letters, each one bubbling with enthusiasm and enterprise. You and Dr. B. Sidney Smith have steered me to the right direction.

Thanks to a special man with iron guts who once wrote to me saying "Everybody knows one thing about me, that there is no agenda hidden behind my writings and I am very vocal and brave. . .therefore I am sidelined by the establishment but so far they could not do anything else. . .." Well, they did do something horrible after all. RIP Syed Saleem Shahzad, the investigative journalist of Asia Times and author of *Inside al Qaeda and the Taliban, beyond 9/11*, tortured and murdered by people yet officially unknown.

Thanks to a few other progressive geniuses with hearts of gold, a genuine compassion towards global suffering, and a common vision towards a better future. I feel exceedingly rich to have read their works, to have tried to understand their opinions about global conflicts and to have assimilated them in my own way. While there are millions of them around the world I am sure, so far I have had the luck to comprehend only a few. In no particular order, they are: Zygmunt Bauman, Tom Engelhardt, Michael T Klare, Patrick and Alexander Cockburn, Michel Chossudovsky, Jason Burke, John Kampfner, Bernd Hamm, James Fishelson, Robert Wirsing, Andrew J Bacevich, Daniel Yergin, William Blum, Mark Zepezauer, Mark Rosenfelder (of zompist.com), Naser Zarafshan, Syed Saleem Shahzad, Nir Rosen, Sami Moubayed, Samir Amin, Zahid Hussain, Ahmed Rashid, Amal Saad-Ghorayeb, M.K. Bhadrakumar, Dilip Hiro, and Prem Shankar Jha.

Thanks to Asia Times Online, Information Clearing House, Counterpunch, Democracy Now!, Global Research, Institute for Economic Democracy, Der Spiegel and Real News Network, for running those extremely crucial blogs, articles, threads, or discussions;

Thanks to Ashok Mitra, KP Nayar, Mukul Kesavan, Kanwal Sibal, Ashok V Desai and SL Rao for your articles and contributions to different print dailies;

Thanks to The Institute for Economic Democracy for expressing the confidence to give this work the tangible shape of a book. Big thanks to Dr Becker Sidney Smith for his meticulous edits and his patience while dealing with me and my mails.

Finally, thanks to you readers—only when you get interested in global affairs do perfect vagabonds like me find a justification to write.

Foreword

I learned about this book when Arindam requested permission to quote from IED's website, ied.org. I was curious about his research and the emerging pattern. Upon reading two sample chapters I was impressed with his understanding of imperialism and plunder by trade'—my tag for globalisation.

This book's focus is a common human vice (greed), and his narrative traverses the world collecting samples of it from concepts, events, and people. Arindam eventually links them all together commendably, and the result rips through the all pervading perception management blanket that keeps reality out of the minds of the masses within the developed world. He pulls no punches to drive the fact that gluttony guided every aspect of plunder throughout colonization or hypercapitalism-derived globalisation. They have been the major systems of theft within capitalism, and whenever there were efforts to address the cause and effect of unearned money, different protection rackets were unleashed throughout modern times. Some demonized Communism and honest societies that tried to walk in the direction of self determination, while some rackets misrepresented Islamic Fundamentalism as monumentally satanic to ensure hypercapitalism's iron grip over Middle Eastern energy resources.

This work is a readable combination of history, international relations, conflicts and economics—the practical version of what is witnessed today whenever NATO airplanes bomb sovereign territories or recession-stuck western governments gear up with bailout packages for the banks.

This book traces the story from western colonial domination, to the United States' ascent to supremacy through gunboat diplomacy and covert and overt warfare. It tracks the pattern of imperialism's efforts to crush socialistic endeavours worldwide, including those in Europe that called for a change in the system of governance. It identifies Jihad as a response to U.S. oppression in the Middle East and other Islamic nations. It takes on oil and gas pipeline politics, it opens up the myth of globalisation, and finally it examines the New World Order and its disorders.

This book is an ideal overview of imperialism and global geopolitics.

When imperialism collapses, Arindam envisions the world reorganizing under honest capitalism. This book, and others like it, will help the world restructure their laws, as applied to nature's resources and technologies, which nature offers to us all for free. Once those laws— the very foundation of the current monopoly structure we are told does not exist—are restructured worldwide to honest capitalism, wars and poverty will only be in history books and civilization will have the resources to mitigate global warming.

I have always believed that there are minds out there that can take our messages and make them many times stronger and more powerful. Arindam's work joins my efforts to provide the foundation for an entire new school of thought. Perception management has been so total for so many centuries, even in academia, that the simple truths behind most of the world's problems are only now being seriously discussed.

This book will bring its readers closer to understanding the causes of today's poverty and wars and thus closer to world peace and the elimination of poverty. Read it, share it with others. This may be the right moment in time for the world to break free and declare, and establish, full and equal rights for every person on earth.

J.W. Smith
Sun City, Arizona, USA, 2011

Dr J.W. Smith is a political economist and the founder of The Institute for Economic Democracy. He is the author of *The World's Wasted Wealth*, *Cooperative Capitalism* (forthcoming), and many other books on the subject of economic democracy.

Setting the Sail — *An Introduction*

> *You've been with the professors, and they've all liked your*
> *   looks*
> *With great lawyers you have discussed lepers and crooks*
> *You've been through all of F. Scott Fitzgerald's books*
> *You're very well read, it's well known*
> *But something's happening here, and you don't know what*
> *   it is*
> *Do you, Mister Jones...?!*
>
> —Bob Dylan, *Ballad of a Thin Man*

This book examines a few crucial events in the history of mankind through the window of a core human vice. This degenerative energy has been discussed many times before, addressed as one would treat a spoilt but loving brat, and has been carefully kept aside to make way for apparently more serious challenges at hand. It has never been taken up for the purpose of fathoming the damage that it has caused to humanity at large through different phases in our economic and political history. It has never been encountered head on, never been checked, never been told "No! Because it is not done." Ever.

Greed—deliberately overlooked and at times encouraged through the ages—has gripped the whole world and has squeezed it slowly and agonizingly. From the old colonizing powers to the relatively new empires that were or are being built as a result of globalisation, nearly every activity has been greed-based: commerce, crusade, or war. And whatever anomalies we see today can be safely attributed to two factors, either the Greed System or the crooks that have come out its shadows.

This incredible task has been achieved historically by the simple act of demolition—of new ideologies or methodologies, sovereign nations or honest leaders or attempts to change—almost anything that has threatened the custodians or the system. Whenever there were marginally more sensible options of trying out newer ideas pertaining to social, political or economic governance, global leaders, mostly slaves to the greed-system, rejected the scope and the forms emphatically.

Through my little experience in the corporate world I have seen that in strategy meetings, if some one tentatively suggests a fresh approach, executives sit up, listen and evaluate. Key ideas that are thought to be potent enough are tried out often. Surprisingly, and contrary to the belief of many, very few ideas are scrapped outright. Organizations work on the understanding of being a singular entity.

Socialism, through the erstwhile USSR, though imperfect in many ways, had brought a viable option to the table. What was expected then was a little honesty on the part of the leaders; to at least give the thought a try across certain pockets. There was a choice of calibration. From geography to ethnicity, from economy to policy making—the leaders had the entire world to choose from for a possible test-market. But the cardinal difference between any average corporate executive and the political leaders lies in the thought process. From Roosevelt to Churchill, from Eisenhower to Bush/Blair, none was sincere enough to visualize the world as a single entity.

The greedsters' historical aversion towards anything that spelt 'common good', and an obsession with control mechanisms, unfortunately has laid down a course the results of which are coming back to haunt us. A decade into the new millennium, we are all painfully aware of the fact that not a single so-called global leader has the required inclination to visualize the world as a single unit—the source of our continuity, our guarantor. The controlling powers have ravaged it through all-pervading trade and war in search for more wealth and more power. As a result of this historic win-lose attitude, while our parents witnessed the imperialists and their colonies, we have the super rich Triad Countries (Chiefly the USA, the EU, Japan, Singapore, South Korea—nations that sit on 50% of the global GDP with only 8% of the global population), their 'friends' (KSA, UAE, Israel, Australia, Turkey) at one end and the dilapidated periphery world at the other to observe, with one thing in common—whenever someone has tried to present a better way, he has been ostracised, dishonoured, dismembered, and often done away with.

From poverty and starvation to environmental degradation, from illiteracy and unemployment to religious fundamentalism, we have inherited a multitude of maladies, something that has been accomplished through years of exploitation of lives and resources—for oil or gas, for forests or minerals, or sometimes just for 'strategic' importance—and these maladies are something that we are going to pass on to our future generations. As time passes by, newer and more complicated conflicts set in and get integrated into the framework of an already super-burdened society.

Through this work I have attempted to uncover the Greed System and have tried to remove the perception management blanket that has been thrown over us by the offenders who, by some irony of fate, have inherited this earth. I hope that very soon an enlightened generation will eventually be instrumental in changing the score: Only there lies our chance for a better future.

Arindam Mukherjee Calcutta 2011

To my wife Razia

1 Greed — *A Curtain Raiser*

All good things were at one time bad things; every original
sin has developed into an original virtue..
   —Friedrich Nietzsche

Whoever loves money never has money enough; whoever
loves wealth is never satisfied with his income.
   —Ecclesiastes 5:10

Greed is defined by Webster as "excessive or rapacious desire, especially for wealth or possessions; avarice; covetousness."

That craving for extra profit, a better car, a bigger diamond, often resorting to unfair means at the expense of others to maximise wealth accumulation, like producing over capacity to earn more at no extra expense—that set of ambitions is nothing but good old greed.

Greed is as old as humanity. We can track it through our civilization's history and records. From as far back as human triumph over animals during the beginning, or in that classical Old Testament action of Adam eating the apple (the blame put squarely on someone else, which is also another remarkable human trait that we will be talking about), or in the more recent example of colonial aggression, greed has always been primary. Curiously enough, greed as a form of negative energy has managed to completely eclipse our brains; most human beings have been successfully programmed to overlook or ignore how greed has been guiding our path for thousands of years.

It was not superior human faculties, as we know, but pure bloodlust that led our ancestors to slaughter animals unnecessarily [roman-colosseum.info], wherever possible, and finally settle on top of the pyramid. It was not just plain curiosity, but desire that made Adam eat that juicy-looking ripe apple. Similarly the Europeans' greed for absolute possession of all the global wealth led to their "Imperial Ambitions" [Chomsky, *Year 501...,* Page 8]. Hunting animals until about yesterday was legitimate, today it is called poaching—and a tiger skin sells for thousands of dollars in black markets in Tibet. Greed for food is prevalent even today (the US even has a "national disease" called obesity)— and these were two small follow-up examples from the start of this paragraph, because since the Stone Age we have travelled along with the flow of greed.

Believed and defended by many as the fuel behind human supremacy, greed when discussed gets mixed up with another term called rational self-interest. Though many left-of-centre people would see no difference between greed and rational self-interest (which is hailed to be the cornerstone of capitalist economies), the objective here is not to start a debate on economics based on the philosophies that one believes in. So to see rational self-interest off on a good note: The difference between rational self-interest and greed is that rational self-interest harnesses desire strictly within the marketplace to build or preserve a robust economy—as long as it remains legitimate, in other words. When the same emotion crosses over to the other side, runs amok, inflates disproportionately and creeps into the value system of an individual or a group, it becomes greed. Carefully controlled and applied with restraint (meaning, as long as it remains within the boundaries of rational self-interest) this emotion can benefit a society. Moderation has never been a threat or curse.

But control has always been a human weakness. We love it. We mess it up too. Many times we think we are in control of things when those things are actually beyond salvation. More often than not, the mask becomes the real face. Jekyll becomes Hyde. Permanently.

In the same manner, greed as a form of energy has grown so disproportionately over the years that today it controls us. This is not surprising. This growth has been partly natural and partly orchestrated. But whatever that method may be, the result is among us. Today's world is lined with greed for two objects: wealth (or material possessions) and power are the ultimate dream acquisitions for all of us around this world—individuals, groups, corporations, politicians, or kings. There is no break in that picture. "More" is the word for most of the things in this world—more money, more fame, more facilities, more advantages. . . it is an exhaustive list. At the start of the 21st century, the world is ideologically bankrupt. There is no visionary assertion of values, goals, and aims. There are no ties to keep people together; there are no rationalizations of what is bigger and more important than each of us. In fact most of us with our super-inflated ego consider ourselves to be God's gift to green Earth—bigger and more important than everything else. There are no theories or speculations, no call for loyalty. Grand, national, or visionary, subdued or local, delivered from the podium or unspoken— ideologies are nowhere to be found [www.g-r-e-e-d.com]. That void has been filled by an increasing narcissism in society, and a greed for material wealth and power. There are no common banners that unite us. We live in a consumer-mad society that is ideally suited to a miniscule proportion of 'nomad elites of global liquid modernity." [Escobar, *Globalistan*] But the point is hardly visible due to the burning-up overdrive that is prevalent everywhere, across every societal strata. If we take a look at our surroundings—physically or through a media-aid, we see a mindless consumption spree. An aspiration to be a glitzy size zero at one end and McBurgers at the other. We see glossy magazines and glossier celebrities, designer brands and lifestyle products—and everything, including an astronomically priced SUV, sounds affordable to our consumerised mind these days. No barrier seems strong or high or intimidating enough. It is a crazy, no holds barred, look-flashy-or-die-trying, wannabe society that is rapidly taking over.

> Present-day consumerism, though, is no longer about satisfying the needs—not even the more sublime, detached (some would say, not quite correctly, 'artificial', 'contrived', 'derivative') needs of identification or the self-assurance as to the degree of 'adequacy'. It has been said that the *spiritus mavens* of consumer activity is no longer the measurable set of articulated needs, but desire—a much more volatile and ephemeral, evasive and capricious, and essentially non-referential entity than 'needs', a self-begotten and self-propelled motive that needs no other justification or 'cause'. [Bauman, *Liquid Modernity*, 74–75]

Do we realize that we are living entangled in a maze of self-deceit? I guess we do not, because if we do, then a horribly ugly world presents itself, once the layers of carefully constructed consumerist ideology peel off.

Talking of ourselves as individuals, there is a clear line between *modernization* and *westernization*. The majority of the developing world, in their disinterest, are indifferent towards such classifications. A vast amount of confusion has crept into the middle-class youths of today's emerging economies when in their greed they have increasingly embraced a crass end of westernization, with more and more atrocious results. Aspirations flow not from time elapsed, lessons learnt, character built or virtues implemented, but from a desire to 'belong'. A low-key element of greed with a massive penetration power across cultures, ethnicities, and geography acts as the most potent post-modern emotion. For example, a large section of Indian youth routinely overhaul their accent or wear hip-hop accessories and walk with a swagger, or crowd at waterholes discussing the latest reality show, while they guzzle down beer. That their ambition in life is to look/sound like an inane someone, anyone, suffering from a hyper dosage of the ghetto culture ideally should be no major concern to anyone, but problems arise when priorities get driven by greed. Yes, if you thought that greed was only about Enron trying to buy the world, think again. Among you and me, greed is about an incredible urge among an incredible number of less-learned individuals buying tangibles or intangibles mindlessly, to belong. From Enron and Lehman Brothers, the other picture of greed is something like Dubai trying to buy culture to look-feel like Rome or Paris. We are millions of miniscule individual Dubais all in our own buying binge, hardly aware of how our consumerism-influenced points of view and subsequent actions contribute substantially to misery and oppression and, if continued this way, even the possible destruction of this world.

And that was just us. What about our leaders, whom we have entrusted with the single most important responsibility of running the world? To look after our welfare and that of our planet?

Simply put, "we" never had the power to entrust, and "they" never needed our permission for anything. First there were monarchs who collected taxes from us and ruled us by brute force. Then societies invented elected representatives. These leaders designed the Greed System in the first place. Then they got progressively greedier, and naturally the system underwent some upgrades. Somewhere down the line, they realised that the common man needed to be insulated from the truth, needed to be barred from asking uncomfortable questions.

Though the deployment of consumerism was to serve the logic of capitalism—to persuade people to buy things they did not need–so that manufacturers could sell more; one kind of greed eventually made way for another, as mesmerised buyers quickly evolved to a stage where they kept demanding a new toy everyday. Around the same time, the "public relations'" industry that was first used to influence public political opinion was quickly fine-tuned to serve the needs of consumerism—to persuade more people to buy. Similarly, the evolution of print or electronic media has not much helped in increasing awareness; it has managed quite the opposite. Consumerism and media, the two initiatives taken by the leaders to upgrade the old Greed System, have thus had a sedative effect on societies. If you are beginning to see a little bit of the picture, let us do some fact-finding ourselves, to get a flavour that drives home the legitimacy of that bit of the picture that you see. Here is authentic progressive reporting, far away from the latest mainstream media buzz that we are normally fed with every day:

> [That] immensely rich veins of gold and copper ore in West Papua led to decades of genocide and environmental destruction, all for the benefit of a cartel of wealthy corporations, has essentially been left out of history books. . .

> The slaughter of one-third of East Timorese citizens in a failed attempt to control what are thought to be vast oil deposits escaped notice until it had failed. . .That same process is going on in Darfur in the Sudan, is addressed as a genocidal disaster, but almost no media mentions who the hidden players are or that the underlying struggle is to control anticipated oil reserves. . .

> Most of the destabilizations we address here were openly over who would control resources and wealth. . . As we outline examples... remember these destabilizations were done by good people just like you and I who believed fully in what they were doing. . . Those carrying out the orders of managers of state had never heard anything other than that they were battling the world's worst elements who were attempting to take away our democratic freedoms [ied.info].

Is it hard to believe that all these atrocities were planned and executed in cold blood, for greed? Welcome to the New World Order, where greed rules all the three elements—New, World, and Order. Where the fate of a nation or people gets decided not by their rightful place on earth, but by their affiliation to the school of greed. Where well-known authors croon through print that the more natural resources you have, the poorer your state of affairs is going to be—so you should give in to the powerful and let them guide you. Where global leaders perform mass-murders without a reason, and where the rest of the people do not have any remorse, because they are too numb—and really comfortable.

The only piece of good news is that not all of us are greedsters. Once you know the score, you have joined the millions of us today who do not approve of what is going on in this world in the name of Liberty, Democracy, or a Free Economy. There are thousands among us who do not trust what our governments say. That is where the silver lining is. For the rest of us first-timers who want to refocus at this point, it is of crucial importance that we take our minds off the latest sedatives—a new gadget, car, or music video—for a little while to try to understand how greed, after initially paving the way for human superiority over animals, has been continuously at work pitting humans against one another through Colonialism or Globalisation; how perception management has given birth to absurd woes like "Communist takeover" or religious fundamentalism; how all of them put together have augmented the cause of major protection rackets; and how these complexities together form a threat that dominates the present and guides future trends.

2 Meet the Parents — *A Short Account of the Lineage*

Man is physically as well as metaphysically a thing of shreds and patches, borrowed unequally from good and bad ancestors. . . .

—Ralph Waldo Emerson

Behind every fortune there's an undiscovered crime.

—Balzac

Before we formally take up the greatest Greedster of the past century, perhaps a brief look at its predecessors would lend us a few advantages. We would understand the lineage—the breed history, and thus the foundation. Then, at points in time, we would also understand how greed, from an energy form, shaped up gradually into an organised and complex system, got a life of its own, infiltrated across all levels of the society to stand as it is today—how the mask became the real face. So, moving back from the United States of America: a nation that has been brought up on a staple of greed, a nation that has worshipped greed, a nation that has successfully exported greed (in fact greed is the most successful US international export of all times, you can forget the "American Dream" tag), and a nation that has taken greed to dizzying heights—let us first take a brief look at this hyper-greedy torchbearer's equally greedy ancestors.

October 11, 1992 brought to an end the 500th year of the Old World Order, sometimes called the Colombian era of world history, or the Vasco da Gama era, depending on which adventurers bent on plunder got there first. Or "the 500-year Reich," to borrow the title of a commemorative volume that compares the methods and ideology of the Nazis with those of the European invaders who subjugated most of the world. The major

theme of this Old World Order was a confrontation between the conquerors and the conquered on a global scale. It has taken various forms
and been given different names: imperialism, colonialism, the North-
South conflict, core-*versus*-periphery—or, more simply, Europe's conquest of the world [Chomsky, *Year 501*, Page 8].

The overall development of individual European nations was going
on, taking its own time as it would back in those days, when there was
this urge among the Spanish traders to find the New World: typically
India, bypassing the Arab middlemen. More profit, in short. As rational
self-interest gradually gave way to greed, Europe in an attempt to feed
it's greed discovered the sea-route to America and to Asian nations, and
commenced the exploitation of natural resources and fairly easily con-
querable peoples. The Great Race (of colonizing the entire world) was
on. The results were unprecedented. Translated into real estate figures,
"By 1900 Great Britain had grabbed 4,500,000 square miles; France had
gobbled up 3,500,000; Germany, 1,000,000; Belgium 900,000; Russia,
500,000; Italy, 185,000; and the United States, 125,000" [Prouty, *JFK*,
236–237]. With these large tracts of land came huge new markets for the
conqueror's manufactured products. Unfortunately a significant chunk
of the colonies made finished goods that were far superior to those that
Europe tried to feed them forcibly. But commercial superiority had to
be established over the poor colonial population. So, after the initial ransacking was over, trade links got consolidated through a maze of political
and commercial embargoes.

Adam Smith wrote in 1776, "The discovery of America and of a passage to the East Indies by the Cape of Good Hope are the two greatest
and most important events recorded in the history of mankind.... What
benefits, or what misfortunes to mankind may hereafter result from those
great events, no human wisdom can foresee" [odur.let.rug.nl]. Mark the
words: "greatest", "most important" and "benefits." For the invaders this
was true, since these events were to cascade a history of unprecedented
wealth accumulation by the Western nations. About "foresee"-ing the
result, what Mr Smith could not visualise then, or thought no "human
wisdom" could imagine, became quite starkly evident soon afterwards to
a lot of human beings—wise or otherwise, especially to the conquered
and the oppressed citizenry of different colonised nations. For them it

was an emphatic series of never ending "misfortunes" and misery spanning hundreds of years.

> The conquest of the New World set off two vast demographic
> catastrophes, unparalleled in history: the virtual destruction of the
> indigenous population of the Western hemisphere, and the devas-
> tation of Africa as the slave trade rapidly expanded to serve the
> needs of the conquerors, and the continent itself was subjugated.
> Much of Asia too suffered "dreadful misfortunes." While modali-
> ties have changed, the fundamental themes of the conquest retain
> their vitality and resilience, and will continue to do so until the re-
> ality and causes of the "savage injustice" are honestly addressed.
> [Chomsky, *Year 501*, 10]

The Pioneers and Their Establishment of Greed Dynamics

As mentioned before, credit goes to the Iberian Peninsula: Spain and
Portugal took the initiative in leading the rest of Europe into the art
and science of high-seas piracy, looting, invasion, slave-trading, and so
on. The issue however, as with most pioneering activity, was that there
was a lack of fine-tuning to a certain extent. So, even though they were
pretty promising beginners in such acts, two key shortcomings that led
to their downfall were: a) they were impatient, and b) they were brain-
less. In their savage eagerness and denseness, they did not spare their
home ground. This came to the surface when they started forcefully con-
verting, expelling, or killing their Jewish community. Millions of Moors
suffered the same fate. Eight Hundred years of Moorish rule disappeared
with the fall of Granada in 1492, because of the Spanish Inquisition.
Though there are two sides to the story as usual, of who was right and
who was wrong—the Moors that captured the Iberian Peninsula, or the
Spanish Reconquista team—the fact still remains that in their medieval-
mindedness, they killed or enslaved some 100,000 Moors and were responsible for another 200,000 emigrating elsewhere. With the fall of
Granada the conquering army of Ferdinand and Isabella went on a ram-
page characteristic of medieval times, destroying books, manuscripts, or
other priceless testimonies of an important civilization. "...The stage was
set for the decline of Spain, and also for the racism and savagery of the
world conquest." [Chomsky, *Year 501*, 11].

The greed-system was moving with an incredible speed and so were the first generation greedsters. As the Spanish-Portuguese duo faltered in the race, competition stepped in and within a short while of their decline the baton of greed was snatched by the Dutch.

If Spain and Portugal's contribution to the dynamics of greed was savagery, Holland was the pioneer in mixing business and politics with savagery. In 1602, the Dutch East India Company was created. Practically it was an extension of the state, replete with the full powers and rights to make war and treaties. That was the beginning of a fashion, one that continues even today: a maze of transnational institutions rich beyond measure, controlling the political landscape of the most advanced nations in an advanced and borderless world [Chomsky, *Year 501*, 11].

The Dutch went from strength to strength and colonised huge stretches of land from Indonesia to India, Brazil, and the Caribbean. Among others, they snatched Sri Lanka from Portugal. They were ideal colonialists, but for a chink in their armour. It was later known as "the Dutch disease," as Chomsky continues, "an inadequate central state power, which left the people 'rich perhaps, as individuals; but weak, as a State,' as Britain's Lord Sheffield observed in the 18th century, warning the British against the same error."

The Dutch issue was a shortage of manpower. Their country was relatively sparsely populated. They later realised that continuous wars, the characteristic of the time then, was not an option. With their military losses, the Dutch started focusing on commerce. So, even as the Anglo-Dutch Trade Wars decreased the Dutch Asian trade, the Dutch domestic infrastructure continued to expand and dominate Europe. With large amounts of capital in both the bank and exchange, European merchants sought more and more Dutch financing. And, as the Dutch saw a quick decline in their military prowess, the Dutch Republic continued to see economic development that would lead towards the Industrial Revolution.

The British took over soon afterwards, sailing under Her Majesty's banner, secretly thankful to the notorious robber, slave-trader, invader, and pirate Sir Francis Drake. During 1579-80, Drake robbed Spanish ships, sacked Chilean ports and attacked Spanish settlements along Pacific South America and collected a huge fortune. Eventually he returned

to England in 1580 with enormous wealth in silver and gold. "Queen
Elizabeth was a considerable shareholder in the syndicate which had financed the expedition. Out of her share she paid off the whole of England's foreign debt, balanced her Budget, and found herself with about
£40,000 in hand. This she invested in the Levant Company—which pros-
pered. Out of the profits of the Levant Company, the East India Company was founded," [www.econ.yale.edu] "the profits of which...were
the main foundations of England's foreign connections." [Chomsky, *Year
501*, 11].

But what was with the rest of the world that they would always give
up without a fight? Or go down fighting, as was the case in many instances? Why would the European colonialists always win wars? It has
been observed that European success was largely a function of their culture of violence. According to John Keay's observation, "Warfare in
India was still a sport. . . in Europe it had become a science." [zcommu-
nications.org]. Factually,

> ...the mathematicians of the Renaissance applied their geometry
> to all manner of practical disciplines.... Developments in the art
> of warfare in the late 15th and 16th centuries provided another
> outlet for geometry, and the mathematicians were quick to re-
> spond by devising techniques, designing instruments and writing
> books. Heavy guns manufactured in single metal castings were
> longer, capable of more accurate fire, and were adjustable in el-
> evation. Consequently, gunners needed instruments to measure
> both the inclination of the barrel and the distance to the target,
> together with a means of relating these two measurements. Ge-
> ometers offered a variety of solutions to these problems, as well
> as designs for fortifications to withstand attack from the new ar-
> tillery. [*The Geometry of War, 1500–1750*]

Instances are many. "Geoffrey Parker points out that 'Cortés conquered Mexico with perhaps 500 Spaniards; Pizarro overthrew the Inca
Empire with less than 200; and the entire Portuguese empire (from Japan
to southern Africa) was administered and defended by less than 10,000
Europeans.'" [Chomsky, *Year 501*, 12–13]. Robert Clive was outnum-
bered nearly ten to one at the Battle of Plassey against Nawab Siraj ud
Daulah of Bengal in 1757, which opened the way to the takeover of Bengal by the East India Company.

Europeans "fought to kill," and they had the means to satisfy their blood lust. In the American colonies, the natives were astonished by the savagery of the Spanish and British. "Meanwhile, on the other side of the world, the peoples of Indonesia were equally appalled by the all-destructive fury of European warfare," Parker adds. Europeans had put far behind them the days described by a 12th century Spanish pilgrim to Mecca, when "The warriors are engaged in their wars, while the people are at ease." The Europeans may have come to trade, but they stayed to conquer: "trade cannot be maintained without war, nor war without trade," one of the Dutch conquerors of the East Indies wrote in 1614 [that] European domination of the world "relied critically upon the constant use of force," Parker writes: "It was thanks to their military superiority, rather than to any social, moral or natural advantage, that the white peoples of the world managed to create and control, however briefly, the first global hegemony in History." [Chomsky, *Year 501*, 13].

Savage merchants consolidated the first three dynamics of global greed. Then, from the creation of the East India Company, the subsequent invasion of different kingdoms of the Indian Peninsula and other foreign lands through the 'science of war,' but more importantly, through continuous maintenance of that huge empire, British Imperialism took the greed dynamics ahead as yet another trait surfaced: sustenance. This was their capability to administer foreign territories through their divide-and-rule and Balkanization policy to ensure protracted control. "Differentiation" and "centralization," says Mohammad J Kuna—"two mechanisms that express and embody processes of the creation and maintenance of boundaries—within and between colonised people and societies" [udusok-ng.academia.edu, *Coloniality and the Geography of Conflicts in Northern Nigeria*]. Soon after overrunning the Nawab of Bengal, the British were able to reduce the numerical odds against them by mobilizing native mercenaries, who constituted ninety percent of the British forces that held India for the next two hundred years. The policy was successfully implemented by mobilizing the same greed-system among the natives. An assured pay package at the end of the week to an otherwise overlooked, mostly unemployed and grossly illiterate section of people—and legitimised acceptance of their existence by the English dominated society albeit as second/third class members—did the job.

Again, towards the latter half of their colonial hegemony, they successfully introduced the Hindu-Muslim divide in India and the Muslim-Jew
divide in Arabia. The carrot was old but the package was new; the lure
of a nation based on religious superiority.

The British contribution finally completed the greed dynamics of the
Old World Order: it was the ability of a nation to exploit/extract/loot
wealth from foreign nation(s) at gun-point, or through other modes of
savagery, in the name of business and commerce. The gun-point bit
was called political administration. Their contribution actually produced
some unparalleled results that neither pure Spanish savagery nor pure
Dutch business relations could ever think of achieving. There have been
robbers and pirates since times immemorial. Similarly, overseas merchants were old hat. In fact they are the ones that set sail first; of course,
with time a lot of them got greedy and the story was never the same
again.

> The plains of North America and Russia are our corn fields;
> Chicago and Odessa our granaries; Canada and the Baltic our tim-
> ber forests; Australia contains our sheep farms, and in Argentina
> and on the Western prairies of North America are our herds of
> oxen; Peru sends her silver, and the gold of South Africa and Aus-
> tralia flows to London; the Hindus and the Chinese grow our tea
> for us, and our coffee, sugar and spice plantations are all in the
> Indies. Spain and France are our vineyards and the Mediterranean
> our fruit garden; and our cotton grounds, which for long have oc-
> cupied the Southern United States, are being extended everywhere
> in the warm regions of the earth [Kennedy, *Rise and Fall of Great
> Powers*, 151–152].

No petty thug or stand-alone trader could build an empire like this
purely out of their profession, let alone sustain it. The English showed
the world for the first time that one needed several angles of operation to
build an empire.

Since we are dealing with greed and its aftershocks, it is perhaps
pertinent in the scope of things that we consider the fate of the colonies.
From the 17th century until now there have been a few more covers and
tags added to greed dynamics, but the result of it on the oppressed remains much the same. The baton of greed might have passed from England to the US, the colonies might have changed names and geographies,

but the situation has not. While this work is chiefly dedicated to study-ing New World Order maladies, let us build the foundation through some authentic observations on the results of Old World Order greed.

By 1700, the East India Company accounted for more than half of British trade. The transformation of the subcontinent was entirely trade-centric. Examine this passage from Dr J.W. Smith's book Cooperative Capitalism:

> After India was conquered, its import and export policies were controlled by Britain, which not only banned Indian textiles from British markets, but also taxed them to a disadvantage within In-dia so British cloth would dominate the Indian market. India's internal production of cloth was not only excluded from their own internal market, so as to be undersold by Britain's inferior cloth, Britain also excluded those beautiful and much higher quality fab-rics from England while marketing them all over Europe.

The results of the Greed System were crucial—they created a di-lapidated peripheral blob that constituted the entire globe outside of the West, what mainstream media terms the "third world."

> The fate of Bengal brings out essential elements of the global conquest. Calcutta and Bangladesh are now the very symbols of misery and despair. In contrast, European warrior-merchants saw Bengal as one of the richest prizes in the world. An early English visitor described it as "a wonderful land, whose richness and abundance neither war, pestilence, nor oppression could de-stroy." Well before, the Moroccan traveler Ibn Battuta had de-scribed Bengal as "a country of great extent, and one in which rice is extremely abundant. Indeed, I have seen no region of the earth in which provisions are so plentiful." In 1757, the same year as Plassey, Clive described the textile center of Dacca as "extensive, populous, and rich as the city of London;" by 1840 its population had fallen from 150,000 to 30,000, Sir Charles Trevelyan testified before the Select Committee of the House of Lords, "and the jun-gle and malaria are fast encroaching. . .Dacca, the Manchester of India, has fallen from a very flourishing town to a very poor and small town [Chomsky, *Year 501*, 17].

This gradual transition of India from a once prosperous nation to a third-world state was achieved through pure torture and trade embargoes that were employed during the Raj. After the British takeover, the Go-moshtas or the native trade-agents deployed by the East India Company to liaise with the local weavers, usually forcibly acquired produce at a fraction of the price. "Force" meant fines, imprisonment, or severe flog-ging depending on circumstances. These issues were occasionally taken up by English authorities (Governor Vansittart) with higher offices in the shape of formal protests, but remained generally overlooked and often encouraged [Hallward, *William Bolts*, 10–18].

In the next phase, the Indian handicraft industry was brought to a halt. This was achieved by secluding India from the reaches of the In-dustrial Revolution and systematically annihilating the industries "by ex-posing them to the ruinous competition from the cheap machine products coming from the UK" [hindubooks.org]; and once they were done with the industrial sector, the British colonialists turned to rural Bengal. In 1779 the English rulers forced the Bengali peasants to cultivate indigo in their paddy lands because there was a great demand for colour dyes in the European market. The problem was that once indigo was planted it took two to three years to mature, and in this time no other crops could be cultivated. Economical loss notwithstanding, this was a huge loss of essential food grain for the country. But whoever refused to cultivate indigo was subjected to the same inhuman torture and oppression.

This went on for the next eighty years or so, before the people of Bengal revolted and the cultivation of indigo stopped. But Bengal was not just about prosperous industries or rice. There was jute and tea which the British merchants cast their greedy eyes on, after the indigo cultiva-tion was on its way. In order to further increase their profits, they fully exploited these two commodities as well. To aid the uninterrupted flow of agricultural wealth, Lord Cornwallis successfully imposed British feu-dalism on the rural economy of Bengal through the system of permanent settlements. In 1793, the infamous Zamindars of Bengal came into the picture once again following the Settlement when, in accordance with the system, the Colonialists armed these greedy counterparts of theirs with enormous economic power, an authority to impose revenue taxes on land, evict farmers, arbitrarily sell farmers' movable and immovable property, and even prosecute farmers and sentence them to death. The exploits of this treacherous Zamindari system is archived in numerous accounts, fictional and non-fictional, in Bengali and Hindi literature. A more contemporary version is of course visible through a later-day study of American puppets and dictators installed across expansive stretches of the so-called Third World. As Chomsky observes, "The oppression and monopolies" imposed by the English "have been the causes of the decline of trade, the decrease of the revenues, and the present ruinous condition of affairs in Bengal"

Those colonies that were longest under the greed pioneers usually were the poorest. J.L. Nehru was of the opinion that "some kind of chart might be drawn up to indicate the close connection between length of British rule and progressive growth of poverty.". In the mid-18th century India was developed by comparative standards, not only in textiles but also in industries like ship building. One of the flagships of an English admiral during the Napoleonic wars was built by an Indian firm. Besides ship-building, there were metal working, glass, paper, and many other medium and small scale crafts that flourished. But all of these declined under British rule, as India's development was arrested and the growth of new industry blocked. It was an effort to marginalise India into an "an agricultural colony of industrial England." And this was achieved brilliantly, so while Europe urbanised, India and other colonies progressively ruralised with an incredible increase in the proportion of the population dependent on agriculture, "India is as much a manufacturing country as an agriculturalist; and he who would seek to reduce her to the position of an agricultural country, seeks to lower her in the scale of civilization. . .." Looks like that was the exact intent of the British Imperialists, and they were rather successful too. [Nehru, *The Discovery of India*, 296–299]

Meet the Offspring

The American colonies were settled by the same (or nearly the same) set of people from England and parts of Europe, and they took the same path laid out by their ancestors. The English had a well-marked three-pronged plan to pursue: Raiding and looting the Spaniards, French, and other European colonialists; decimating the native Indians; and controlling the seas through home-bred pirates to as far as the Arabian Sea. Building settlements was a concern sure, but the greed for wealth and real estate acquisition was way ahead in terms of priorities. The first years of colonization saw Virginia as their base. They used this place to raid Spanish commerce and for marauding French settlements on the coast of Maine. They also used this place as a launch-pad to "exterminate the 'devil worshipers' and 'cruel beasts' whose generosity had enabled the colonists to survive, hunting them down with savage dogs, massacring women and children, destroying crops, spreading smallpox with infected blankets, and other measures that readily came to the minds of barbarians fresh from their Irish exploits" [Chomsky, *Year 501*, 28]. During the first onslaught three types of people were dealt with permanently— the native Indians, who were not 'civilised,' and the more advanced and vastly superior natives of Peru and Mexico. These people were completely annihilated. Hugo Grotius, a leading 17th century humanist and the founder of modern international law, determined that the "most just war is against savage beasts, the next against men who are like beasts" [Thorup, *The Horror of the 'Enemy of Humanity'*, 9]. This, from the founder of "modern" international law. No wonder George Bush could crave Saddam Hussein and eventually get him on a platter. The trend was set way back in 1783 actually, when one of the founding fathers of the US, George Washington, wrote that "the gradual extension of our settlements will as certainly cause the savage, as the wolf, to retire; both being beasts of prey, tho' they differ in shape" [Washington, *Letter to James Duane*, 1783]. So do not be surprised if in the near future someone uncovers that Hugo Grotius considered these immortal words the basis, among other philosophies, of international law.

Respected statesmen upheld the same values even scores of years later, statesmen like Theodore Roosevelt. According to him "the most ultimately righteous of all wars is a war with savages," especially the ones that led to the establishment of "the dominant world races" [Theodore Roosevelt, *The winning of the West: Book IV*]. In November 1864 a group of around 700 volunteers under Col. Chivington, a Methodist preacher, massacred a Cheyenne and Arapaho settlement in Big Sandy Creek, Colorado at the crack of dawn, without any warning, killing and mutilating hundreds of unarmed men, women, and children. This was done chiefly to drive the natives out of the territory following the discovery of gold in Colorado. A preacher in his mission for gold, maiming people and leaving them to die! But to Mr. Roosevelt, this was "as righteous and beneficial a deed as ever took place on the frontier" [apfn.org]. With leading humanists, poets, preachers, and respected leaders—it was a list comprised of an ever-increasing and widespread mix of occupations—people from all possible societal strata each with their own agenda were quick to get in on the morally-endorsed quest for fortune.

Theodore Roosevelt was a noble-minded man. Or so we know. Every book heaps praises on him. Many contemporary ideologues of today worship him as a hero. This same visionary,

> did not limit his vision to the "beasts of prey" who were being swept from their lairs within the "natural boundaries" of the American nation. The ranks of savages included the "dagos" to the south, and the "Malay bandits" and "Chinese half-breeds" who were resisting the American conquest of the Philippines, all "savages, barbarians, a wild and ignorant people, Apaches, Sioux, Chinese boxers," as their resistance amply demonstrated [Chomsky, *Year 501*, 31].

An overseas concordance at a much later date and in a different context comes from Winston Churchill, who "felt that poison gas was just right for use against 'uncivilised tribes' (Kurds and Afghans, particularly). Noting approvingly that British diplomacy had prevented the 1932 disarmament convention from banning bombardment of civilians, the equally respected statesman Lloyd George observed that 'we insisted on reserving the right to bomb niggers,' capturing the basic point succinctly" [Chomsky, *Year 501*, 31]. So Americans demonstrated unbridled savagery towards the beginning of their life cycle—a trait that was an important first, in order of priority. Spaniards did that a few hundred years ago. The Colonisers were intelligent learners. They would later on implement the full spectrum of greed dynamics—step by step, all in good time.

Charity begins at home
The US grew up rather fast. After ransacking the native Indians and pushing the Spaniards and French into the hinterland or down south, with no imminent threat or hazard in sight, consolidating on permanent establishments became the core focus. A few years down the line, the settlers

discovered that wars were unnecessary expense at times, so they graduated to acquiring the natives' land by fraud, tricks, threats, etc. would
predict to John Adams that the "backward" tribes at the borders "will
relapse into barbarism and misery, lose numbers by war and want, and
we shall be obliged to drive them, with the beasts of the forests into the
Stony mountains" [www.loc.gov]. The same would be true of Canada
after the conquest he envisioned, while all blacks would be removed to
Africa or the Caribbean, leaving the country without "blot or mixture"
[Chomsky, *Year 501*, 29].

Things went generally well for them. To get rid of dark corners
in their geography, to aid civilization and minimise unwanted intrusion,
trees and Indians were regularly mowed down. Both would yield readily.
Gradually, the shape of the enemy transformed. In a change of events,
England became Enemy No. 1 and remained much-hated among a huge
section of people, rich or poor, for its demand on the American colonies
for its own debt reduction. The western hemisphere witnessed the signs
of a "great" nation in the making during the middle of the 18th century,
when the savage youngster started showing tendencies of being grown-
up enough to challenge the alpha male of the pack. The climax was
achieved though the War for Independence.

Love thy neighbour: dismembering Mexico
But even after winning the first war against England, Americans were
intensely aware that England's military force was too powerful to con-
front in the long run. The Grand Strategy of Britain was actually to
keep an iron grip on the industry and markets of the American colonies.
The practical version of it was that not even a common nail was to be
produced in America, and under no circumstances were manufactured
products to be exported to countries within Britain's trade empire. It
was visible immediately after America's independence, when England's
Lord Brougham proposed destroying America's infant industries by sell-
ing manufactured goods to them below cost [ied.info]. That was one
threat. On the other side, Spain and France were continuing to be a de-
terrent despite being flogged regularly. To counter these threats once and
for all, Jacksonian Democrats called for annexation of Texas (which was
otherwise a part of Mexico before the Texan Revolution), to gain a global

monopoly of cotton. The objective was to paralyze England and intimidate Europe. While defenders of American behaviour would argue about the cause-and-effect cycle, in this practical version of eat-or-be-eaten, greed was gradually surfacing as the emerging winner. No one bothered. So, the hungry offspring resorted to organised war to invade and annex Texas, California and New Mexico. The year was 1846. Some scholars believe that at the base of such action was an American thought of creating their own Grand Strategy, copying Britain's neo-mercantilist trade policy [Dorfer, *America's Grand Strategy*, 16].

Salutations flooded the government houses of this new country. "By securing the virtual monopoly of the cotton plant" the US had acquired "a greater influence over the affairs of the world than would be found in armies however strong, or navies however numerous," President Tyler himself observed after the invasion and conquest of nearly half of Mexico. The objectives were not clear though. Whether it was for commercial monopoly, a lust for blood, or for the pure pleasure of watching other people suffer, the great leader could not clarify. So we can safely assume all of the above and read on, because the picture does not change much. Mr Tyler wrote "An embargo of a single year would produce in Europe a greater amount of suffering than a fifty years' war. I doubt whether Great Britain could avoid convulsions." The same idea was endorsed by top administrators, governors, newspapers, and the like, in different styles. All concluded that it was a great start and that the US was to conquer the global trade system within the next fifty years if the going went the same way. A governor proclaimed an immediate 'mastery of the Pacific' to further strangle European resources. In other words, to introduce organised and legitimised high-seas pirates [Chomsky, *Year 501*, 34].

The USA was a promising offspring. Its extraordinary potential was noticed from the earliest days, and of no small concern to the guardians of established order. There were many concerns expressed both tacitly and elaborately around many corners of Europe. The Czar and his diplomats were concerned over "the contagion of revolutionary principles," which "is arrested by neither distance nor physical obstacles.. . ." [Chomsky, *Year 501*, 34]. Likewise, there was a new fear of a "flood of evil doctrines and pernicious examples," (a phrase is attributed to Klemens von Metternich, a 19th century Austrian diplomat much admired by such modern western strategists as Henry Kissinger) and people wondered "what would become of our religious institutions, of the moral force of our governments, and of that conservative system which has saved Europe from complete dissolution" if the USA was to advance unhindered [Kennedy, David, and Thomas Bailey, *The American Spirit: Volume 1*, 276].

Thus the new leader of the pack. And what about the Mexicans? The American national poet, Walt Whitman, wrote: "What has miserable, inefficient Mexico... (got) to do with the great mission of peopling the New World with a noble race?" [smithsoniansource.org]. And apart from the great national poet, "(O)thers recognised the difficulty of taking Mexico's resources without burdening themselves with its 'imbecile' population, 'degraded' by 'the amalgamation of races,' although the New York press was hopeful that their fate would be "similar to that of the Indians of this country—the race, before a century rolls over us, will become extinct" [Chomsky, *Year 501*, 34–35]. That was in the 18th century, so naturally the people sounded uncouth and embarrassingly loud. Soon the US would contribute to greed dynamics the incredible muffling power of media—the biggest paradox of both the modern and post-modern world.

Through brutality and exclusivity, the greed-system demonstrated its effect on the human psyche, and possibly one of the most important examples was laid down through America's violent ascent—long before the advent of modern day financial speculations or free market systems. But no one was bothered. Savagery, invasion, and occupation—the checklist of greed dynamics—did their part in the "rounding out of the natural boundaries" [chomsky.info]. Protracted control of the peripheries as well as other sovereign nations was to follow next.

3 Masters of the World — *The 20ᵗʰ Century Greedster*

Do not remove the ancient landmark
   that your ancestors set up.

   —Bible: Hebrew, Proverbs 22:28

What can one say about a country where a museum of science in a great city can feature an exhibit in which people fire machine guns from a helicopter at Vietnamese huts, with a light flashing when a hit is scored? What can one say about a country where such an idea can even be considered?

   —Noam Chomsky

In 1823 President James Monroe instituted a policy that later came to be known as the Monroe Doctrine, which proclaimed that Latin America from then was out of bounds for European Imperialism [future.state.gov]. And, in 1837, after a section of the US supported a rebellion in Canada against British Imperialism, and the English forces in response crossed the border and set fire to the US vessel Caroline, Secretary of State Daniel Webster promulgated another doctrine that was later to become the foundation of modern international law. It argued that "respect for the inviolable character of the territory of independent states is the most essential foundation of civilization," and force may be used only in self defence, when the necessity "is instant, overwhelming and leaving no other choice of means, and no moment of deliberation" [Chomsky, *Year 501*, 32].

These are two key doctrines, one intended to limit the European sphere of influence and the other intended to protect the integrity of a sovereign nation. On the face of it, these were good initiatives. Even the Latin Americans rallied behind the Monroe Doctrine at the start. But for the US the reason for limiting the European sphere of influence was diametrically opposite to the Latin American perception. From the very beginning of the North American colonies there was an unceasing "rounding out of the natural boundaries" of their territory, as a result of which, by the end of the 19th century, the US extended to the mid-Pacific. With or as a result of its military success, or just because of pure self-adulation of being Anglo-Saxon and thus a superior race, a common belief that the western hemisphere was their dominion was gradually building and was starting to manifest among the new US elites. The Monroe Doctrine was a sign that many outsiders did not understand. The Americans' perception of the extent of the US's natural boundary was growing significantly bigger with time—thus the 'natural boundaries' of the South also had to be defended. To manifest and sustain the expansion planning and initiatives were necessary—and the Monroe Doctrine was just the beginning. It was of little concern whether the Latin Americans or anyone rallied behind them or not.

So what was (and is) the role of the South after all? A contemporary account by the esteemed linguist Noam Chomsky, of what the South still does for the US, gives us an idea. The actual amount of revenue earned in dollars, minerals mined, petroleum drilled, drugs peddled or financial scams perpetrated can never be fathomed. We can hope for some WikiLeaks type whistleblower that deals in history to give us some clue in the near future. But for now, let us not be surprised if it is known tomorrow that US wealth interests in South and Latin America can make a chunk of European Colonialist fraternity look like little jokers of the Indian Circus in their polka dotted tunics.

> The South is assigned a service role: to provide resources, cheap labour, markets, opportunities for investment and, lately, export of pollution. For the past half-century, the US has shouldered the responsibility for protecting the interests of the "satisfied nations" whose power places them "above the rest," the "rich men dwelling at peace within their habitations" to whom "the government of the world must be entrusted," as Winston Churchill put the matter after World War II [Chomsky, *Year 501*, 43].

For the Americans, the southern peripheral area was huge, the resources were plenty, and stakes were high. An urge to dominate and control these satellite states was the Imperialistic fashion during those days. And for the US policymakers looking for an excuse, the ascent of the Bolsheviks immediately during the time succeeding the First World War provided them one: threats of an imminent Communistic takeover.

> The primary threat to these interests is depicted in high-level planning documents as "radical and nationalistic regimes" that are responsive to popular pressures for "immediate improvement in the low living standards of the masses" and development for domestic needs. These tendencies conflict with the demand for "a political and economic climate conducive to private investment," with adequate repatriation of profits (NSC 5432/1, 1954) and "protection of our raw materials" (George Kennan). For such reasons, as was recognised in 1948 by the clear-sighted head of the State Department Policy Planning staff, "We should cease to talk about vague and...unreal objectives such as human rights, the raising of the living standards, and democratization," and must "deal in straight power concepts," not "hampered by idealistic slogans" about "altruism and world-benefaction," if we are to maintain the "position of disparity" that separates our enormous wealth from the poverty of others (Kennan) [Chomsky, *Year 501*, 43].

With time and the decline of Communism, the United States' leadership developed a new smokescreen to rationalise greed; we will look through that sometime later.

Historically we of course observe that the US needed no reason to maul its southern neighbours, it was considered to be their birthright. But what did the Daniel Webster's doctrine say by the way? That "respect for the inviolable character of the territory of independent states is the most essential foundation of civilization" [thirdworldtraveler.com]. Let us now take a look at how the founding nation of so esteemed a doctrine has honoured the principle since the early 19th century.

Uncle Sam in Latin America
The following pages contain a timeline of US interventions in Latin America adapted from a compilation by Mark Rosenfelder at zompist.com. (Used by permission.) As we review this record we should keep two things in mind: The unfortunate and ill-fated southern neighbours

of the US have borne US atrocities through all the years of their common history. Second, this chronology is absolutely vital to understand the United States' idea and intent about absolute control of the world. Yes, greed has that effect on nations and people.

MEXICO: The country that suffers from the simple misfortune of being the US's southern border.

> 1846 The US, fulfilling the doctrine of Manifest Destiny, goes to war with Mexico and ends up with a third of Mexico's territory. And what was the Manifest Destiny all about? It was a self righteous belief of the settling US Anglo-Saxons that it was their divine expansionist right to own and rule the whole of the American continent.

> 1905 US Marines help Mexican dictator Porfirio Díaz crush a strike in Sonora.

> 1914 US bombs and then occupies Vera Cruz.
>
> During World War I, the US also invaded Mexico and Hispaniola (present day Dominican Republic and Haiti).

> 1917 US troops enter Mexico to catch and kill Pancho Villa. They fail.

NICARAGUA: British and United States interests in Nicaragua grew during the mid-1800s because of the country's strategic importance as a transit route across the isthmus connecting North and South America.

> 1854 The US navy bombs and destroys the Nicaraguan port town of San Juan del Norte. Some sites say that the attack occurred after US millionaire Cornelius Vanderbilt sailed his yacht into the port and an official attempted to levy charges on his boat [internationalpeaceandconflict.org], and some other sites mention that it was the US response after a Minister of theirs was 'insulted.'

> 1855 William Walker, operating on behalf of bankers Morgan & Garrison, makes entry into Nicaragua and soon proclaims

himself President and restores slavery.   He is promptly
recognised by the US. He remains President so long as he
complies to US interests.   When he cuts off the leash, he is
toppled, exiled, and ultimately executed [internationalpeace-
andconflict.org].

1909 Dollar diplomacy protectorate set up.   Known as "[a] policy aimed at furthering the interests of the United States
abroad by encouraging the investment of US capital in foreign countries" [Wikipedia], this was a plain buy-out of foreign governments that the US deemed fit for its interests.

1909 Liberal President José Santos Zelaya of Nicaragua is forced
to resign through pressure after the US lands 400 marines
on the country to threaten the government for the execution
of two US mercenaries by President Zelaya. Jose' Madriz is
appointed as the President. He would resign after a year.

1911 The new president is Adolfo Díaz, described as "empty—
headed as a drum, who was employed at a salary of eighty
dollars a month, as bookkeeper in the La Luz and Los An-
geles Mining Company [Arevalo, *The Shark and the Sar-
dines*]." He is of course backed by the US.

1912 US marines invade Nicaragua, to muscle up the inept Díaz
government against contender General Luis Mena, beginning an occupation that was to last almost continuously until 1933. An election is called in 1913, to resolve the crisis:
there are thousands of eligible voters, and one candidate,
Díaz. The US maintains troops and advisors in the country
until 1925. In the same year, President Taft declares: "The
day is not far distant when three Stars & Stripes at three
equidistant points will mark our territory: one at the North
Pole, another at the Panama Canal and the third at the South
Pole. The whole hemisphere will be ours in fact as, by virtue
of our superiority of race, it already is ours morally" [inter-
nationalpeaceandconflict.org].

1926 Marines, out of Nicaragua for less than a year, occupy
      the country again, to settle a political situation. Secretary
      of State Kellogg describes a "Nicaraguan-Mexican-Soviet"
      conspiracy to inspire a "Mexican-Bolshevist hegemony" in
      Nicaragua. His anxiety is apparent after a leftist party wins
      elections in Mexico, which is a familiar trend in Latin Amer-
      ica then, which is again a result of protracted US atrocities.
      More and more liberal leftist regimes, though not in power
      were experiencing a huge surge in popular support among
      people.

1929 the US establishes a military academy in Nicaragua to train
      a National Guard as the country's army. Similar forces are
      trained in Haiti and the Dominican Republic.

> There is no room for any outside influence other than
> ours in this region. We could not tolerate such a
> thing without incurring grave risks.. . . Until now Cen-
> tral America has always understood that governments
> which we recognise and support stay in power, while
> those which we do not recognise and support fall.
> Nicaragua has become a test case. It is difficult to
> see how we can afford to be defeated. (Recording of
> Undersecretary of State Robert Olds.)

1933 Marines finally leave Nicaragua, unable to suppress the
      guerrilla warfare of General Augusto César Sandino They
      leave dictator Anastasio Somoza and his National Guard in
      control. Somoza becomes the first Nicaraguan commander
      of the National Guard.

1934 Sandino assassinated by agents of Somoza, with US ap-
      proval. Somoza assumes the presidency of Nicaragua two
      years later. In a surprising show of integrity and respect to-
      wards the Monroe Doctrine, Secretary of State Cordell Hull
      explains, to block his ascent would be to intervene in the
      internal affairs of Nicaragua.

> After Somoza García won in the December 1936 pres-
> idential elections, he diligently proceeded to consol-

idate his power within the National Guard, while at
the same time dividing his political opponents. Family members and close associates were given key positions within the government and the military. The
Somoza family also controlled the PLN, which in
turn controlled the legislature and judicial system,
thus giving Somoza García absolute power over every sphere of Nicaraguan politics. Nominal political opposition was allowed as long as it did not
threaten the ruling elite. Somoza García's National
Guard repressed serious political opposition and anti-
government demonstrations. The institutional power
of the National Guard grew in most government-
owned enterprises, until eventually it controlled the
national radio and telegraph networks, the postal and
immigration services, health services, the internal revenue service, and the national railroads. In less than
two years after his election, Somoza García, defying
the Conservative Party, declared his intention to stay
in power beyond his presidential term. Thus, in 1938
Somoza García named a Constituent Assembly that
gave the president extensive power and elected him
for another eight-year term.

Somoza García's opportunistic support of the Allies during World War II benefited Nicaragua by in-
jecting desperately needed United States funds into
the economy and increasing military capabilities.
Nicaragua received relatively large amounts of military aid and enthusiastically integrated its economy
into the wartime hemispheric economic plan, providing raw materials in support of the Allied war effort.
Exports of timber, gold, and cotton soared. However,
because more than 90 percent of all exports went to
the United States, the growth in trade also increased
the country's economic and political dependence.

Somoza García built an immense fortune for himself
and his family during the 1940s through substantial
investments in agricultural exports, especially in cof-
fee and cattle. The government confiscated German
properties and then sold them to Somoza García and
his family at ridiculously low prices. Among his many

industrial enterprises, Somoza García owned textile
companies, sugar mills, rum distilleries, the merchant
marine lines, the national Nicaraguan Airlines (Líneas
Aéreas de Nicaragua-Lanica), and La Salud dairy—
the country's only pasteurised milk facility. Somoza
García also gained large profits from economic concessions to national and foreign companies, bribes,
and illegal exports. By the end of World War II, Somoza García had amassed one of the largest fortunes
in the region—an estimated US$60 million. (Merrill,
Tim. Nicaragua: A Country Study. Claitors Pub.,
1995.)

Special Mention: "Somoza may be a son of a bitch, but he's
our son of a bitch."—F.D. Roosevelt, President of the US.

1979 Nicaragua gains its freedom on July 19, when the Sandinista liberation forces overthrow President Somoza. Under
the guidelines of NSC—68, American managers of state immediately make plans to reverse that revolution [ied.info].

The new government inherited a country in ruins, with
a stagnant economy and a debt of about US$1.6 bil-
lion. An estimated 50,000 Nicaraguans were dead,
120,000 were exiles in neighbouring countries, and
600,000 were homeless. Food and fuel supplies were
exhausted and international relief organizations were
trying to deal with disease caused by lack of health
supplies. [countrystudies.us]

1981 The Reagan Administration initiates the "contra war"
against the Sandinista government in Nicaragua. Claiming
that Nicaragua, with assistance from Cuba and the Soviet
Union, is supplying arms to the guerrillas in El Salvador,
the Reagan administration suspends all United States aid
to Nicaragua and later that year, the administration authorises support for groups trying to overthrow the Sandinistas.
An initial budget of US$19 million, camps in southern Hon-
duras as a staging area is approved. The US also sets up an
economic embargo of Nicaragua and pressures the IMF and

the World Bank to limit or halt loans to Nicaragua. Boland Amendment prohibits CIA and Defense Dept. from spending money to overthrow the government of Nicaragua—a law the Reagan administration cheerfully violates.

1984   CIA mines three Nicaraguan harbours. Nicaragua takes this action to the World Court, which brings an $18 billion judgment against the US The US refuses to recognise the Court's jurisdiction in the case.

1990   Massive US intervention in the Nicaraguan election process through covert and overt means. Washington openly funds the opposition coalition though such foreign funding of US parties was illegal under US law.

Special Mention: The resulting bloodshed was perhaps the least covert of all CIA covert operations. President Reagan was perfectly candid about the goals; the second-poorest nation in the hemisphere was to be "pressured" until "they say 'uncle'" [Zepezauer, *The CIA's Greatest Hits*].

The Nicaraguan government was protecting its citizens under the Sandinistas. The improvement in education, health, and living standards under the Sandinistas was reversed by the destabilization process of the US interventions. Massive US funds illegally financed the opposition and the harassed Sandinistas finally agreed to an election. As expected, the American-backed Violeta Chammoro became president of Nicaragua in February 1990. Though Chammoro was not the thief and oppressor that Somoza had been, the suffering nation that was once rapidly progressing under the Sandinistas went on to become one of the poorest nations of Latin America as their resources again started feeding the industries and populations of the imperial centers of capital [ied.info].

CUBA: Ah, Cuba! The only nation in the US's vicinity that dared to profess its neutrality, and later incorporated nationalist policies under Fidel Castro.

1783 The second US president, John Adams, expressed what was to be the US's attitude towards Cuba until the end of the 19th century. He said the island was a natural extension of the North American continent, and that the continuation of the United States made its annexation necessary [easynet.co.uk].

1898 The US declares war on Spain, blaming it for destruction of the battleship USS Maine. The war enables the US to occupy Cuba, Puerto Rico, Guam, and the Philippines. Over 80 years later, US Admiral G.H. Rickover admitted that the Spanish had not blown up the Maine, and actually US 'specialists' had set the explosives on board. The majority of the 260 US crew killed were black, the white officers having been ashore at the time [easynet.co.uk].

1901 US forces leave Cuba and the country gains its" independence" only after passage of the infamous Platt Amendment that gets inserted into the Cuban constitution granting the US the right to intervene in Cuba's internal affairs at any time. Cuba is also forced to cede Gauntanamo Bay to the US, in perpetuity. Cuba emerges as the model for US imperialism—that of securing American Economic and Political Domination without the seizure of a colony. This unique model gives United States the moral right to boast its anti-colonial tradition and beliefs. It is at this time that the term 'sphere of influence' becomes an international euphemism for neo-colonialism [easynet.co.uk].

1906 Marines occupy Cuba for two years.

1909 Another US intervention in Cuba

1912 US Marines intervene again in Cuba

1917 Yet another Marine intervention again in Cuba—this time, to guarantee sugar exports during World War I.

1917–23 The US kept holding on to Cuba when Russian Revolution inspired an upturn.

1933 President Roosevelt announces the Good Neighbour Pol-
      icy, opposing any armed intervention in Latin America, and
      probably to celebrate the announcements, he sends 20 war-
      ships to Cuba to intimidate Gerardo 'The Butcher' Machado
      Morales, a one—time US puppet, who is massacring the
      people to put down nationwide strikes and riots. Machado
      resigns. The first provisional government lasts only 17
      days; the second Roosevelt finds too left-wing and refuses
      to recognise. A pro-Machado counter-coup is put down by
      Fulgencio Batista, who with Roosevelt's blessing becomes
      Cuba's new strongman.

1959 Fidel Castro takes power in Cuba.

1960 Eisenhower authorises covert actions to get rid of Castro.
      Among other things, the CIA tries assassinating him with
      exploding cigars and poisoned milkshakes. Other covert ac-
      tions against Cuba include burning sugar fields, blowing up
      boats in Cuban harbours, and sabotaging industrial equip-
      ment.

1961 Bay of Pigs. The US organises force of 1400 anti-Castro
      Cubans, ships it to the Bahía de los Cochinos. Castro's army
      routs it.

      Title 18 of the US Code declares it to be a crime to launch a
      "military or naval expedition or enterprise" from the United
      States against a country with which the United States is not
      (officially) at war. So, Attorney General Robert Kennedy
      had determined after the Bay of Pigs that the invasion did not
      constitute a military expedition [Blum, *Killing Hope, Part 1*,
      188].

      The Bay of Pigs planners had made a major mistake of as-
      suming that the Cuban people would rise up to join the in-
      vaders. There was probably a belief in the American es-
      tablishment that the ordinary Cubans would view the Cuban
      Revolution in a negative light and respond to the overture
      of capitalist America spontaneously. When the Bay of Pigs

ended shamefully, the establishment went into overdrive to cause serious damage to the Cuban economy and politics through sea or air or commando raids, assassinations, bombing of vessels, pirate attacks on fishing boats, off shore shelling, and so on [Blum, *Killing Hope, Part 1*, 187–188].

During the sixties, these clandestine raids were coupled with a complete US trade and credit ban, which continues to this day. And the US administration is pretty obstinate about it too. For example, "...when Cuba was hard hit by a hurricane in October 1963, and Casa Cuba, a New York social club, raised a large quantity of clothing for relief, the United States refused to grant it an export license on the grounds that such shipment was 'contrary to the national interest'" [Blum, *Killing Hope, Part 1*, 187].

What else could the great US do to bring the Cubans down on their knees? They coerced other countries to ban trade with Cuba. While Ronald Reagan would probably have wanted to pressure them until they cried "uncle," back then Kennedy was in no mood to establish family ties. The Bay of Pigs slap still burnt the cheek. So "goods destined for Cuba were sabotaged: machinery damaged, chemicals added to lubricating fluids to cause rapid wear on diesel engines, a manufacturer in West Germany paid to produce ball-bearings off-centre, another to do the same with balanced wheel gears—'You're talking about big money,' said a CIA officer involved in the sabotage efforts, 'when you ask a manufacturer to go along with you on that kind of project because he has to reset his whole mould. And he is probably going to worry about the effect on future business. You might have to pay him several hundred thousand dollars or more'" [Blum, *Killing Hope, Part 1*, 188].

1969–70 The CIA deployed futuristic weather modification technology to ravage Cuba's sugar crop and undermine the economy. Planes from the China Lake Naval Weapons Center in the California desert fly over Cuba seeding rain clouds with crystals that precipitate torrential rains over non-agricultural areas and leave the cane fields arid [thirdworldtraveler.com].

1971 CIA infects Cuba with a virus that causes African swine fever. Six weeks later, an outbreak of the disease in Cuba forces the slaughter of 500,000 pigs to prevent a nationwide animal epidemic.

1996 The US battles global Communism by extending most-favoured-nation trading status for China, and tightening the trade embargo on Castro's Cuba.

HONDURAS. The original "banana republic" courtesy of the US. A back-water tropic, turned into a banana plantation area and romping ground for the US army and a training base for Contra forces that the US used to attack the Sandinista government of Nicaragua.

1905 US troops land in Honduras for the first of 5 times in the next 20 years.

1907 Marines intervene in Honduras to settle a war with Nicaragua.

1911 The Liberal regime of Miguel Dávila in Honduras over-thrown by former president Manuel Bonilla, aided by Amer-ican banana tycoon Sam Zemurray and American merce-nary Lee Christmas, who becomes commander-in-chief of the Honduran army.

1943 The editor of the Honduran opposition paper El Cronista is summoned to the US embassy and told that criticism of the dictator Tiburcio Carías Andino is damaging to the war ef-fort. Shortly afterward, the paper is shut down by the gov-ernment.

1980s The US, seeking a stable base for its actions in El Salvador and Nicaragua, starts pouring in $100 million of aid a year and basing the contras on Honduran territory.

EL SALVADOR. Nothing special. Just that those oppressed, poor and famine-ridden people wanted to achieve betterment through self-determination—they wanted to choose their own government.

1932   The US rushes warships to El Salvador in response to a popular communist rising. President Martínez, however, prefers to put down the rebellion with his own forces, killing over 8000 people.

> It was found unnecessary for the United States forces and British forces to land," US Chief of Naval Operations Admiral William V. Pratt testified before Congress, "as the Salvadoran Government had the situation in hand." Martinez was granted informal recognition at once on the grounds of his success in "having put down the recent disorders" (State Department). . ..
>
> The effectiveness of the Matanza at suppressing dissent was indicated by the passage of over a generation before rural organizing began again. As late as 1978 a reporter quoted a conservative lawyer who stated, 'Whenever the peasants make the least demand, people start talking about 1932 again" [Chomsky, *Turning the Tide*, 74. 152].

1944   The dictator Maximiliano Hernández Martínez of El Salvador is ousted by a revolution; the interim government is overthrown five months later by the dictator's former chief of police. The US immediately recognises the new dictator.

1960   A new junta in El Salvador promises free elections; Eisenhower, fearing leftist tendencies, withholds recognition. A more attractive right-wing counter-coup comes along in three months.

"Governments of the civil-military type of El Salvador are the most effective in containing communist penetration in Latin America."—John F. Kennedy, after the coup

1963 The US government sends 10 Special Forces personnel to El Salvador to help General Jose Alberto Medrano set up Organizacion Democratica Nacionalist (Orden)—first paramilitary death squad in that country. These green berets assist in organization and indoctrination of rural"civic" squads that gathers intelligence and later on carries out political assassinations in coordination with the Salvadoran military.

1968 Gen. José Alberto Medrano, who is on the payroll of the CIA, organises the ORDEN paramilitary force, considered the precursor of El Salvador's death squads. By 1969, some 300,000 Salvadoran (one in eight) citizens flee to Honduras for a living.

1972 The US stands by as the military suspend an election in El Salvador in which centrist José Napoleón Duarte was favoured to win.

1980 A right-wing junta takes over in El Salvador. The US begins massively supporting the government, assisting the military in its fight against FMLN guerrillas. Death squads proliferate. 35,000 civilians are killed in 1980–83.

"The Soviet Union underlies all the unrest that is going on."—Ronald Reagan

1981–83 Colonel Carranza, leader of Salvador's infamous Treasury Police, oversaw the government reign of terror in which 800 people were killed each month.

Carranza received $90,000 a year from the CIA from 1979–84. Reportedly living in Kentucky [The Nation, 6/5/1988, 780].

1984 The US spends $10 million to orchestrate elections in El Salvador.

Special Mention—

Playboy Magazine: Do the American military advisers also tell you how to run the war?

Duarte: This is the problem, no? The root of this problem is that the aid is given under such conditions that its
use is really decided by the Americans and not by us. Decisions like how many planes or helicopters we buy, how
we spend our money, how many trucks we need, how many
bullets and of what caliber, how many pairs of boots and
where our priorities should be—all of that ... And all the
money is spent over there. We never even see a penny of
it, because everything arrives here already paid for [www-
personal.umich.edu/Īormand].

The United Nations El Salvador Truth Commission's 1993
report placed responsibility for 85% of the 70,000-plus
deaths on security forces trained, armed, and advised by the
American military and another 10% upon the El Salvadoran
elite's private death squads which was in effect the brainchild of American governments. The protracted suppression
was successful from the point of US administration, and El
Salvador still remains a provider of cheap resources and labor to the imperialist center of the world.

PANAMA. The US needed a canal to connect the two oceans.

1903 When negotiations with Colombia break down, the United
      States sends warships to back a rebellion in Panama in or-
      der to acquire the land for the Panama Canal. US en-
      couraged separate state of Panama is created. The French-
      man Philippe Bunau-Varilla negotiates the Canal Treaty and
      writes Panama's constitution. Colombia was later paid $25
      million in compensation.

1908 US troops intervene in Panama for the first of 4 times in the
      next decade.

1918 US Marines occupy Panamanian province of Chiriqui.

1925 US Army troops occupy Panama City.

1936 The US relinquishes rights to unilateral intervention in
      Panama.

1941 Ricardo Adolfo de la Guardia deposes Panamanian president Arias in a military coup—first clearing it with the US Ambassador.

It was "a great relief to us, because Arias had been very troublesome and very pro-Nazi."—Secretary of War, Henry Stimson

1946 The US Army School of the Americas opens in Panama as a hemisphere-wide military academy. Its linchpin is the doctrine of National Security, by which the chief threat to a nation is internal subversion; this will be the guiding principle behind dictatorships in Brazil, Argentina, Uruguay, Chile, Central America, and elsewhere.

1981 Gen. Torrijos of Panama is killed in a plane crash. There is a suspicion of CIA involvement, due to Torrijos' nationalism and friendly relations with Cuba. John Perkins in his later day book Confessions of an Economic Hit Man alleges that CIA organised operatives had planted a bomb in the aircraft [Perkins, *Confessions of an Economic Hit Man*, 156–157].

1987 Nationalist movement gets ousted in Panama. Over 2000 people are slaughtered and key leaders arrested.

1989 The US invades Panama to dislodge CIA boy-gone-wrong Manuel Noriega, an event which marks the evolution of the US's favourite excuse from Communism to drugs. This operation also leaves thousands of civilian casualties.

ECUADOR. A copybook case of covert interventions in which the CIA's created "leftist" organizations that condemned poverty, disease, illiteracy, capitalism, and the United States thereby attracted committed militants and their money away from legitimate leftist organizations.

1960–63 Almost all political organizations of significance, from the far left to the far right, get infiltrated during this phase. The

CIA manipulates the entire nation, by planting phoney anti-communist news items in cooperating newspapers, planting false documents on people coming from Cuba—to highlight the communistic threat of the Cuba/Soviet takeover of Ecuador, bombing churches or right-wing organizations and making it appear to be the work of leftists, marching in left-wing parades, and displaying signs and shouting slogans of a very provocative anti-military nature, designed to antagonise the armed forces, forcing them to lash back. They even take the Presidential physician Dr Felipe Ovalle in their payroll [Blum, *Killing Hope, Part 1*, 153–155].

1961   After two years of relentless acts of subversion, the CIA-backed coup overthrows elected President J. M. Velasco Ibarra.

1963   The Presidential Palace in Quito is surrounded by tanks and troops. Arosemana is out, a junta is in. Their first act is to outlaw communism; "communists" and other "extreme" leftists are rounded up and jailed, the arrests campaign being facilitated by data from the CIA's Subversive Control Watch List [Blum, *Killing Hope, Part 1*, 155–156].

1964   Civil liberties are suspended, the elections are canceled—a familiar story that repeats many times in Latin America.

DOMINICAN REPUBLIC. The US did the noble job of saving democracy from communism by getting rid of democracy in this country [Blum, *Killing Hope, Part 1*, 155–156].

1904–05   The US sends customs agents to take over finances of the Dominican Republic to assure payment of its external debt. President Theodore Roosevelt declares the United States to be "the policeman" of the Caribbean; the Dominican Republic is then found to have committed an offence and is placed under a "customs receivership" [internationalpeaceandconflict.org].

1916 Marines occupy the Dominican Republic, staying until 1924.

1930 Rafael Leonidas Trujillo emerges from the US—trained National Guard to become dictator of the Dominican Republic.

1961 Trujillo gets assassinated, by CIA intervention.

Special Mention — "There are three possibilities, in descending order of preference: a decent democratic regime, a continuation of the Trujillo regime or a Castro regime. We ought to aim at the first but we really can't renounce the second until we are sure we can avoid the third." President John F Kennedy [netwar.wordpress.com].

1962 Elections are held, under terms dictated in large part by US Ambassador Martin to the two major candidates. His purpose is to introduce into the Dominican Republic some of the features that Americans regard necessary, inescapably a highly condescending intrusion into the affairs of a supposedly sovereign nation. His instructions extend down to the level of what the loser should say in his concession speech [Blum, *Killing Hope, Part 1*, 178].

1963 CIA-backed coup overthrows elected social democrat Juan Bosch in the Dominican Republic.

1965 A popular uprising in the Dominican Republic attempts to restore Bosch's government. So US President Johnson sends around 20,000 soldiers to "restore order." Johnson acts in the stated belief that the Constitutionalists were dominated by communists and that they therefore could not be allowed to come to power, another example of US invasion and occupation to stop "Communist rebellion,"—the fifth landing of US Marines in that century [iciss.ca].

GUATEMALA. Jacobo Arbenz, elected president of Guatemala, hoped to transform Guatemala " 'from a backward country with a predominantly feudal economy to a modern capitalist state;' the CIA, however, weighed in heavily on the side of feudalism" [Zepezauer, *The CIA's greatest hits*].

1921   President Coolidge strongly suggests the overthrow of Guatemalan President Carlos Herrera, in the interests of United Fruit. The Guatemalans comply.

1952   Jacobo Arbenz Guzmán, elected president of Guatemala, introduces land reform and in course of time, seizes some idle lands of United Fruit—proposing to pay for them the value United Fruit claimed on its tax returns. The company declared value of $525,000 in tax returns, but wants nearly $16 million for the land. Arbenz refuses to pay such an exorbitant sum. US plan of overthrowing him, which was on ever since Arbenz came into power a year ago through free elections, starts consolidating.

United Fruit was "a state within a state. It owned the country's telephone and telegraph facilities. . .only important Atlantic harbour. . .A subsidiary of the company owned nearly every mile of railroad track in the country." Add to that the relations with America's power elite—"it had close ties to the Dulles brothers, various State Department officials, congressmen, the American Ambassador to the United Nations, and others. Anne Whitman, the wife of the company's public relations director, was President Eisenhower's personal secretary. Under-secretary of State (and formerly Director of the CIA) Walter Bedell Smith was seeking an executive position with United Fruit at the same time he was helping to plan the coup. He was later named to the company's board of directors". So, a coup was the least the US administration could plan [Blum, *Killing Hope, Part 1*, 74].

1954   Dwight Eisenhower, John Foster Dulles and Allen Dulles announce that the (legally-elected) government of Jacobo Arbenz is "communist," therefore must go. The same gets orchestrated by the US administration. The US's handpicked dictator, Carlos Castillo Armas, outlaws political parties, reduces the franchise, and establishes the death penalty for strikers, as well as undoes Arbenz's land reform. In the years that follow nearly 200,000 people lose their lives.

"This is the first instance in history where a Communist government has been replaced by a free one."—Richard Nixon

The preparations were impressive. Especially since an earlier coup attempt, with the CIA backing the remnant colonial elite with money and arms failed, the operatives had to be doubly sure. Initiatives included parachute dropping of Soviet-made arms into Guatemala to be found and support the claim of a Communist takeover, refusal of World Bank loans, USIA's creation of over 200 perception management articles on Guatemala and providing them to Latin American newspapers for anonymous use. That apart, over 100,000 pamphlets titled "Chronology of Communism in Guatemala" and 27,000 copies of anticommunist cartoons and posters were distributed. The USIA produced three perception management movies on Guatemala. Seven weeks before the successful coup, the CIA launched a clandestine radio misinformation campaign.

It was a neat set-up. And when the time was right, with the right proportion of bedlam and chaos ignited among the Guatemalans, fighter aircraft bombed oil and ammunition dumps, strafed Guatemala City, and dropped smoke bombs to make it appear the attack was even larger. The Guatemalan Army fell for the bluff. Apprehending a communist takeover, they forced Arbenz to resign [ied.info].

1960 Guatemalan officers attempt to overthrow the regime of Presidente Fuentes; Eisenhower stations warships and 2000 Marines offshore. Fuentes puts down the revolt.

1960s US Green Berets train Guatemalan army in counterinsurgency techniques. Guatemalan efforts against its insurgents include aerial bombing, scorched-earth assaults on towns suspected of aiding the rebels, and death squads, which kills

20,000 people between 1966 and 1976. US Army Col. John Webber claims that it was at his instigation that "the technique of counter-terror had been implemented by the army."

"If it is necessary to turn the country into a cemetery in order to pacify it, I will not hesitate to do so." —President Carlos Arana Osorio

1963 A far-right–wing coup in Guatemala, apparently US-supported, forestalls elections in which "extreme leftist" Juan José Arévalo was favoured to win.

"It is difficult to develop stable and democratic government [in Guatemala], because so many of the nation's Indians are illiterate and superstitious."—School textbook, 1964

1966 The US sends arms, advisors, and Green Berets to Guatemala to implement a counterinsurgency campaign.

1982 A coup brings Gen. Efraín Ríos Montt to power in Guatemala, and gives the Reagan administration the opportunity to increase military aid. Ríos Montt's evangelical beliefs do not prevent him from accelerating the counterinsurgency campaign.

> As the slaughter of the indigenous population by the Guatemalan military approached virtual genocide, Ronald Reagan and his officials, while lauding the assassins as forward-looking democrats, informed Congress that the US would provide arms "to reinforce the improvement in the human rights situation following the 1982 coup" that installed Ríos Montt, perhaps the greatest killer of them all. The primary means by which Guatemala obtained US military equipment, however, was commercial sales licensed by the Department of Commerce, the General Accounting Office of Congress observed, putting aside the international network that is always ready to exterminate the beasts of the field and forest if there are profits to be made [Chomsky, *Year 501*].

1983 Another coup in Guatemala replaces Ríos Montt. The new President, Oscar Mejía Víctores, was trained by the US and seems to have cleared his coup beforehand with US authorities.

SPECIAL MENTION — "From 1982 to 1983—while Gramajo was Army Vice Chief of Staff and director of the Army General Staff—the Guatemalan military killed 75,000 people and destroyed some 440 villages in a massive counterinsurgency campaign directed primarily against the country's Mayan inhabitants" [harvardwarcriminals.blogspot.com].

"Héctor Gramajo, was rewarded for his contributions to genocide in the highlands with a fellowship to Harvard's John F. Kennedy School of Government". — Noam Chomsky

"Harvard makes mistakes too, you know. Kissinger taught there." —Woody Allen, *Annie Hall.*

CHILE

1958 Salvador Allende misses winning a free election by only 3% votes. US administration, apprehensive of his 'communist" orientation undertakes a massive covert campaign to oust him in the next election of 1964.

1964 The operation turns out to be a huge success. Allende gets only 39% votes and loses the election.

> What was there about Salvador Allende that warranted all this feverish activity? What threat did he represent, this man against whom the great technical and economic resources of the world's most powerful nation were brought to bear? Allende was a man whose political program, as described by the Senate committee report, was to "redistribute income (two percent of the population received 46 percent of the income] and reshape the Chilean economy, beginning with the nationalization of major industries, especially the copper companies; greatly expanded agrarian reform; and expanded relations with socialist and

communist countries" [Blum, *Killing Hope, Part 1*, 209].

1970 Salvador Allende elected in Chile. The CIA provides covert financial support for Allende's opponents, both during and after his election.

SPECIAL MENTION—'The United States had seven weeks to prevent him from taking office. On 15 September, President Nixon met with Kissinger, CIA Director Richard Helms, and Attorney General John Mitchell.   Helms' handwritten notes of the meeting have become famous: 'One in 10 chance perhaps, but save Chile!...not concerned with risks involved...$10,000,000 available, more if necessary...make the economy scream. . .' " [Blum, *Killing Hope, Part 1*, 210].

1971–73 US cuts off ALL foreign assistance and exports to Chile, from food to clothing to spare parts. Even cigarette becomes a rarity in the country.

> "Not a nut or bolt [will] be allowed to reach Chile under Allende," warned then-American Ambassador Edward Korry before the confirmation. The Chilean economy, so extraordinarily dependent upon the United States, was the country's soft underbelly, easy to pound. Over the next three years, new US government assistance programs for Chile plummeted almost to the vanishing point; similarly with loans from the US Export-Import Bank and the Inter-American Development Bank, in which the United States held what amounted to a veto; and the World Bank made no new loans at all to Chile during 1971–73. US government financial assistance or guarantees to American private investment in Chile were cut back sharply and American businesses were given the word to tighten the economic noose [Blum, *Killing Hope, Part 1*, 212].

At least half the population suffer from malnutrition, and around 600,000 children are mentally retarded because they could not get proteins and micronutrients during the first eight months of their lives.

Across the other side,

> (T)he managers of state embargoed Chile and the CIA and America's military, primarily the Navy, coordinated plans for Allende's overthrow. This included picking Chilean military personnel for training at the School of the Americas, then in Panama, and later in Fort Benning, Georgia, then renamed to the Center for Inter-American Security Cooperation, but properly nicknamed The School of Assassins or School of Coups.
>
> Among those handpicked recruits would be dependable supporters for a coup when the time was ripe. Guns used to assassinate President Allende were proven to have been given to the assassins by the CIA which then must abide by the rules of plausible denial and disclaim any responsibility [ied.info].

1973 A US-supported military coup kills Allende and brings Augusto Pinochet Ugarte to power. Pinochet imprisons well over a hundred thousand Chileans (torture and rape are the usual methods of interrogation), terminates civil liberties, abolishes unions, extends the work week to 48 hours, and reverses Allende's land reforms.

> Since the overthrow of Allende, Chile is trumpeted as a great success story of Adam Smith free trade. But...in statistics, where you start and where you quit is everything. After Allende's overthrow, national output dropped 15%, the unemployment rate rose to 20%, wage reductions averaged 15%, and that low level provides the base for most statistics... In 1986, 16 years after Allende's overthrow, Chile's GDP had only regained that 1970 level, real wages were still below that year's level, and per-capita consumption was 15% lower, some calculate 23% lower. Between 1985 and 1990, the income of the top 10% of Chileans rose 90% while the share of Chile's wealth for the

poorest 25% fell from 11% to 7%. The percentage share of national income going to labour dropped from 47.7% in 1970 to 19% 20 years later... The real story of Chile and other emerging nations is that the earnings of labourers declined significantly, their rights declined rapidly, the earnings of the already wealthy climbed astronomically, and the natural wealth of Chile and the rest of Latin America were being rapidly claimed by the imperial centres of capital, a classic example of a successful neo-mercantilist policy [ied.info].

HAITI

1915 US Marines occupy Haiti to restore order, and establish a protectorate which lasts for the next twenty years until 1935

1934 The president of Haiti is barred from the US Officers' Club in Port-au-Prince, because he is black.

SPECIAL MENTION —"Think of it—niggers speaking French!" (Secretary of State William Jennings Bryan, briefed on the Haitian situation.)

1959 US Marines intervene to bail out Francois Papa Doc from a few rebels that sailed from Cuba. Haiti had the dubious distinction of being the poorest of Lat Am nations, because of Papa Doc's tyrannies, but US interest in him was only to preserve the nation from becoming 'communist'

1971 Papa Doc dies and his 19-year-old son, called Baby Doc, becomes "president-for-life."

1986 It becomes apparent that Baby Doc's presidency could not in fact be sustained for his entire life (unless he died soon), so the Reagan administration airlifts him to a retirement villa in France and starts talking about the "democratic process". But, throughout the blood-drenched rule of the Duvaliers, where nearly 100,000 were killed by the Tontons Macoutes

(Duvaliers' private terrorist force) alone, the US barely uttered a peep about human rights violations [Zepezauer, *The CIA's greatest hits*].

2004 Removal of democratically elected Haitian President Aristide, troops occupy the country again. CIA, later leaks a "psychological profile" that paints the courageous, dedicated Aristide as a "psychopath" [Zepezauer, *The CIA's greatest hits*].

BONUS PICKS

1962 CIA engages in campaign in Brazil to keep Jo
     ao Goulart from achieving control of Congress.

1964 João Goulart of Brazil proposes agrarian reform, nationalization of oil. Ousted by the US—supported military coup, the preparations of which started from 1961. US commercial interest turns the country into the most treacherous dictator nation in Latin America for the next 20 years.

1967 A team of Green Berets is sent to Bolivia to help find and assassinate Che Guevara.

1973 Military takes power in Uruguay, supported by the US. The subsequent repression reportedly features the world's highest percentage of the population imprisoned for political reasons.

1983 US troops take over tiny Granada. Rather oddly, it intervenes shortly after a coup has overthrown the previous, socialist leader. One of the justifications for the action is the building of a new airport with Cuban help, which Granada claimed was for tourism and Reagan argued was for Soviet use. Later the US announces plans to finish the airport—to develop tourism.

2000 As part of the "War on Drugs," the US launches Plan Colombia, a massive civil and military aid programme for a country with perhaps the worst human rights record in the hemisphere. Total US funding is $1.3 bn, with 83 percent of that going to the military. Plan Colombia later becomes subsumed into the War on Terror.

2002 Failed US-sponsored coup attempt to depose left-populist President Hugo Chavez in Venezuela.

SPECIAL MENTION — "But this man is a terrific danger and the United States, this is our sphere of influence and we can't let this happen...We have the Monroe Doctrine. We have other doctrines that we have announced. And without question this is a dangerous enemy to our south, controlling a huge pool of oil...We have the ability to take him out, and I think the time has come that we exercise that ability." —Pat Robertson's comments calling for the assassination of Venezuelan President Hugo Chavez [handsofvenezuela.org].

Uncle Sam goes to the Middle East

The previous pages amply illustrates the United States' intent-action pattern in reverent service to Daniel Webster's doctrine. But to stop here and think that the US has been active chiefly around its backyard—and to draw lines around Latin America—would be to overlook the reality that to the US Administration the whole world is the US's birthright, its backyard. And it just does cannot help fiddling around in Latin America when the whole planet is left. Marking Latin America had more to do with those natural territorial ambitions that have historically been associated with animal behaviour. And America has been the top dog of the last century. Yes, there was money to be made—billions of it, so there was trade that needed to be insured and protected; maybe there also was a need to shock-and-awe the world through demonstrating US intelligence and military muscle, but American interest in Latin America would still probably stand out as the sanctimonious act of rounding out its natural boundaries in the Western Hemisphere. For Latin America was certainly not about the control of world power. The Middle East was.

The words 'Middle East' are exchangeable with 'oil'—the key to modern-day energy needs. The following chronology has been adapted from Information Clearing House (www.informationclearinghouse.info) with permission. This timeline "illustrates the lengths to which the US has gone to gain and maintain their domination of the Middle East" because of all that oil and gas below—a region "considered key to the United States' standing as an imperialist world power." It should be noted that this is a partial chronology, and does not document every act of American domination and exploitation of this region.

The web page (informationclearinghouse, article 6308) categorises the chronology into four parts: the United States in search of a foothold in the Middle East, gradual expansion in the region through coups and client states, Soviet invasion of Afghanistan, and the United States' increased interventions after the fall of the USSR The present crisis, known as the "long war" or the "war against terror," which started after 9/11, has been left out—that will be examined in the subsequent chapters.

PART I: Breaking into the Middle East and the fight for oil

1920–28 The US pressures Britain, then the dominant Middle East power, into signing a "Red Line Agreement" providing that Middle Eastern oil will not be developed by any single power without the participation of the others. Standard Oil and Mobil obtain shares of the Iraq Petroleum Company.

1932–34 Oil is discovered in Bahrain, Saudi Arabia and Kuwait, and US oil companies obtain concessions.

1944 A US State Department memo refers to Middle Eastern oil as "a stupendous source of strategic power, and one of the greatest material prizes in world history." During US-British negotiations over the control of Middle Eastern oil, President Roosevelt sketches out a map of the Middle East and tells the British Ambassador, "Persian oil is yours. We share the oil of Iraq and Kuwait. As for Saudi Arabian oil, it's ours." On August 8, 1944, the Anglo-American Petroleum Agreement is signed, splitting Middle Eastern oil between the US and Britain.

Between 1948 and 1960, Western capital earns $12.8 billion in profits from the production, refining and sale of middle eastern oil, on fixed investments totaling $1.3 billion.

PART II: Coups and Interventions, the US's forté

1946 President Harry Truman threatens to drop a "super-bomb" on the Soviet Union if it does not withdraw from Kurdestan and Azerbaijan in northern Iran.

1947 The US helps push through a UN resolution partitioning Palestine into a Zionist state and an Arab state, giving the Zionist authorities control of 54% of the land. At that time Jewish settlers were about 1/3 of the population.

1948 War breaks out between the newly proclaimed state of Israel, and Egypt, Iraq, Jordan and Syria, who had moved troops into Palestine to oppose the partition of Palestine. Israeli force attacks some 800,000 Palestinians, (which was) nearly two-thirds of the population. The Palestinians flee into exile in Lebanon, Jordan, Syria, Gaza, and the West Bank. Israel seizes 77%t of historic Palestine. The US quickly recognises the legitimacy of new boundaries of Israel.

1949 CIA backs a military coup overthrowing the elected government of Syria and establishes a military dictatorship under Colonel Za'im.

1952 US-led military alliance expands into the Middle East with Turkey's admission to NATO.

1953 The CIA organises a coup overthrowing the Mossadeq government of Iran after Mossadeq nationalises Iran's own oil and oilfields to prevent being robbed by British holdings.

The Shah, Mohammed Reza Pahlavi, is put on the throne. He rules as an absolute monarch for the next 25 years. This time goes down in history as one of the worst stretches Iran ever faced because of the Shah's torturing, killing and imprisoning his political opponents.

> In 1976, Amnesty International concluded that the Shah's CIA-trained security force, SAVAK, had the worst human rights record on the planet, and that the number and variety of torture techniques the CIA had taught SAVAK were "beyond belief" [Zepezauer, *The CIA's greatest hits*].

Through the intervention, the United States however manages to wrest control of 40 percent of its share of Iranian oil from Britain.

1955 The US installs a powerful radar system in Turkey to spy on the Soviet Union.

1956 After Egypt's nationalist leader, Gamal Abdul Nasser, receives arms from the Soviet Union, the US withdraws promised funding for the Aswan Dam, Egypt's main development project. A week later Nasser nationalises the Suez Canal to fund the project. In October Britain, France and Israel invade Egypt to retake the Suez Canal. President Eisenhower threatens to use nuclear weapons if the Soviet Union intervenes on Egypt's side; and at the same time, the US asserts its regional dominance by forcing Britain, France and Israel to withdraw from Egypt.

1956 A planned CIA coup to overthrow a nationalist government in Syria, perceived by the United States as 'communist' is aborted because it was scheduled for the same day Israel, Britain and France invade Egypt.

1957 Congress approves the Eisenhower Doctrine, stating "the United States regards as vital to the national interest and world peace the preservation of the independence and integrity of the nations of the Middle East." Another backyard opens up for the United States following the Monroe Doctrine and Truman Doctrine. The Middle East gets tagged along with Latin America.

1957   After anti-government rioting breaks out in Jordan, the US rushes the Sixth fleet to the eastern Mediterranean and lands a battalion of Marines in Lebanon to "prepare for possible future intervention in Jordan." Later that year, the CIA begins making secret payments of millions a year to Jordan's King Hussein. This lasts for the next twenty years, and includes supply of female companions too, as the CIA assumes a new role.

1957–58   Kermit Roosevelt, the CIA agent in charge of the 1953 coup in Iran, plots, without success, to overthrow Egypt's Nasser. "Between July 1957 and October 1958, the Egyptian and Syrian governments and media announced the uncovering of what appear to be at least eight separate conspiracies to overthrow one or the other government, to assassinate Nasser, and/or prevent the expected merger of the two countries" [Blum, *Killing Hope, Part 1*, 89].

1958   The merger of Syria and Egypt into the "United Arab Republic," the overthrow of the pro-US King Feisal II in Iraq by nationalist military officers, and the outbreak of anti-government/anti-US rioting in Lebanon, where the CIA had helped install President Camille Chamoun and keep him in power, leads the US to dispatch 70 naval vessels, hundreds of aircraft and 14,000 Marines to Lebanon to preserve "stability." The US threatens to use nuclear weapons if the Lebanese army resists, and to prevent an Iraqi move into the oilfields of Kuwait, and draws up secret plans for a joint invasion of Iraq with Turkey. The plan is shelved after the Soviet Union threatens to intervene.

1960   The US works to covertly undermine the new government of Iraq by supporting anti-government Kurdish rebels and by attempting, unsuccessfully, to assassinate Iraq's leader, Abdul Karim Qassim, an army general who had restored relations with the Soviet Union and lifted the ban on Iraq's Communist Party.

1963   The US supports a coup by the Ba'ath Party (soon to be headed by Saddam Hussein) to overthrow the Qassim regime, including by giving the Ba'ath names of communists to murder. "Armed with the names and whereabouts of individual communists, the national guards carried out summary executions. Communists held in detention...were dragged out of prison and shot without a hearing...[B]y the end of the rule of the Ba'ath, its terror campaign had claimed the lives of an estimated 3,000 to 5,000 communists."

1966   The US sells its first jet bombers to Israel, breaking with 1956 decision not to sell arms to the Zionist state.

1967   With US weapons and support, the Israeli military launches the so-called "Six Day War," seizing the remaining 23 percent of historic Palestine—the West Bank, Gaza, and East Jerusalem—along with Egypt's Sinai Peninsula and Syria's Golan Heights.

1970   With US and Israeli backing, Jordanian troops attack Palestinian guerrilla camps, while Jordan's US-supplied air force drops napalm from above. The US deploys the aircraft carrier Independence and six destroyers off the coast of Lebanon and readies troops in Turkey to support the assault. The US threatens to use nuclear weapons against the Soviet Union if it intervenes. 5000 Palestinians are killed and 20,000 wounded. This massacre comes to be known as "Black September."

1973   The US rushes $2.2 billion in emergency military aid to Israel after Egypt and Syria attack to regain the Golan Heights and Sinai. The US puts forces on alert, and moves them into the region. When the Soviet Union threatens to intervene to prevent the destruction of Egypt's 3rd Army by Israel, US nuclear forces go to DEFCON III to force the Soviets to back down.

1973–1975 The US supports Kurdish rebels in Iraq in order to strengthen Iran and weaken the then pro-Soviet Iraqi regime. When Iran and Iraq cut a deal, the US withdraws support, denies the Kurds refuge in Iran, and stands by while the Iraqi government kills many Kurdish people.

1979–84 The US supports paramilitary forces to undermine the government of South Yemen, which was allied with the Soviet Union.

PART III: The fall of the Shah and the Soviet invasion of Afghanistan

1978 As the Iranian revolution begins against the hated Shah, the US continues to support him "without reservation" and urges him to act forcefully against the masses. In August 1978, some 400 Iranians are burned to death in the Rex Theatre in Abadan after police chain and lock the exit doors. On September 8, 10,000 anti-Shah demonstrators are massacred at Teheran's Jaleh Square.

1979 The US tries, without success, to organise a military coup to save the Shah. In January, the Shah is forced to flee and the reactionary Shi-ite Islamists led by Ayatollah Khomeini take power in February.

1979 The US publicly supports the Khomeini regime's efforts to suppress the Kurdish liberation struggle and maintain Iranian domination of Kurdistan.

1979 US President Jimmy Carter designates the Persian Gulf a vital US interest and declares the US will go to war to ensure the flow of oil.

1979   In response to Soviet military manoeuvres on Iran's northern border, Carter secretly puts US forces on nuclear alert and warns the Soviets they will be used if the Soviets intervene.

1979   The US begins arming and organizing Islamic fundamentalist "Mujaheedins" in Afghanistan. National Security Advisor Zbigniew Brzezinski writes, "This aid was going to induce a Soviet military intervention," drawing the Soviets into an Afghan quagmire. Over the next decade the US alone passed more than $3 billion in arms and aid to the Mujaheedins, with another $3 billion provided by the US ally Saudi Arabia.

1979   Islamic militants, backed by the Khomeini regime, seize the US embassy in Teheran and demand the US return the Shah to Iran for trial. The Embassy and 52 US personnel are held for 444 days; this international embarrassment prompts new US actions against Iran—including an abortive rescue attempt.

1979   Soviet troops invade Afghanistan—which the US rulers considered a "buffer state" between the Soviet Union to the north and the strategically important states of Iran and Pakistan to the south. The invading force overthrows the Amin government and installs a more pro-Soviet regime.

1980   The US begins organizing a "Rapid Deployment Force," increasing its naval presence and pre-positioning military equipment and supplies. It also steps up aid to reactionary client states such as Turkey, Pakistan and Saudi Arabia. On September 12, Turkey's military seizes power and unleashes a brutal clampdown on revolutionaries and Kurds struggling for liberation in order to "stabilise" the country as a key US ally.

1980   As the Carter administration tries to bully Iran into surrendering the US hostages, supporters of presidential candidate Ronald Reagan cut a secret deal with the Islamic

Republic. "When Ronald Reagan was running for president against Jimmy Carter in 1980, 52 American hostages were being held in Iran. The Reagan/Bush campaign feared that if the hostages were released before the November election, the resulting 'October surprise' might help Carter win...According to former Iranian President Bani-Sadr, Reagan officials met with the Iranians in Paris in October 1980 and gave them $40 million in exchange for agreeing to hold the hostages until after the election. Some sources say former CIA Director George Bush and/or future CIA Director William Casey attended those meetings" [Zepezauer, *The CIA's greatest hits*].

1980 Iraq invades Iran with tacit US support, starting a bloody eight-year war. The US supports both sides in the war providing arms, money, intelligence, and political support to both Iran and Iraq in order to prolong the war and weaken both sides, while trying to draw both countries into the US orbit.

1981 The US holds military manoeuvres off the coast of Libya to bully the Qaddafi government. When a Libyan plane fires a missile at US planes penetrating Libyan airspace, two Libyan planes are shot down.

1981 The Reagan administration secretly encourages Israel and other allies, such as South Korea and Turkey, to ship hundreds of millions of US-made arms to Iran despite a ban on the shipment of US-made weapons.

1981–82 Forces led by the Union of Iranian Communists, Sarbederan, mount an historic resistance to the Islamic Republic; the uprising at Amol at the end of January 1982 is brutally crushed by the forces of the Islamic Republic.

1982 After receiving a "green light" from the US, Israel invades Lebanon to crush Palestinian and other anti-US and anti-Israeli forces. Over 20,000 Lebanese and Palestinians are killed, and Israel seizes southern Lebanon, holding it until 2000.

1982   Lebanon's pro-US President-elect, Bashir al-Jumayyil, is assassinated. The following day, Israeli forces occupy West Beirut, and from 16 to 18 September, the Phalangist militia, with the support of Israel's military under future Prime Minister Ariel Sharon, move into the Sabra and Shatila refugee camps and barbarically massacre over 1,000 unarmed Palestinian men, women, and children.

1983   The US sends troops to Lebanon, supposedly as part of a multinational "peace-keeping" operation but in reality to protect US interests, including Israel's occupation forces. US troops are withdrawn after a suicide bomber destroys a US Marine barracks.

1983   CIA helps murder Gen. Ahmed Dlimi, a prominent Moroccan Army commander who seeks to overthrow the pro-US Moroccan monarchy.

1983   The US provides the Islamic Republic of Iran with a list of Soviet agents.

1984   The US shoots down two Iranian jets over the Persian Gulf.

1985–86   The US secretly ships weapons to Iran, including 1,000 TOW anti-tank missiles, Hawk missile parts, and Hawk radars. The weapons are exchanged for US hostages in Lebanon, and in hopes of increased US leverage in Iran. The secret plot collapses when it is publicly revealed on November 3, 1986, by the Lebanese magazine, Al-Shiraa.

1985   The US attempts to assassinate Sheikh Mohammed Hussein Fadlallah, a Lebanese Shiite leader, 80 people are killed in the unsuccessful attempt.

1986   When a bomb goes off in a Berlin nightclub and kills two Americans, the US blames Libya's Qaddafi. US bombers strike Libyan military facilities, residential areas of Tripoli and Benghazi, and Qaddafi's house, killing 101 people, including Qaddafi's adopted daughter.

1987   The US Navy is dispatched to the Persian Gulf to prevent Iran from cutting off Iraq's oil shipments. During these patrols, a US ship shoots down an Iranian civilian airliner, killing all 290 on board.

1988   The Iraqi regime launches mass poison gas attacks on Kurds, killing thousands and bulldozing many villages. The US responds by increasing its support for the Iraqi regime.

1988   A cease-fire ends the Iran-Iraq war with neither side victorious. Over 1 million Iranians and Iraqis are killed during the 8-year war.

1989   The last Soviet troops leave Afghanistan. The war, fuelled by US-Soviet rivalry, tears Afghanistan apart, killing more than one million Afghans and forcing one–third of the population to flee into refugee camps. More than 15,000 Soviet soldiers die in the war.

1990   April Glaspie, US Ambassador to Iraq, meets with Saddam Hussein who threatens military action against Kuwait for overproducing its oil quota, slant drilling for oil in Iraqi territory, and encroaching on their territory—seriously harming war weakened Iraq. Glaspie reportedly replies, "We have no opinion on the Arab-Arab conflicts, like your border disagreement with Kuwait"—thus giving Saddam a silent nod on his planned invasion of Kuwait.

1990   Iraq invades Kuwait. The US seizes the moment to assert its hegemony in the post-Soviet world and strengthen its grip on the Persian Gulf: the US condemns Iraq, rejects a diplomatic settlement, imposes sanctions, and prepares for an all-out military assault on Iraq.

PART IV: The US's playground in a USSR-less "free world"

1991 After a six month military build-up, the United States led coalition launches" Operation Desert Storm." For the next 42 days, US and allied planes pound Iraq, dropping 88,000 tons of bombs, systematically targeting and largely destroying its electrical and water systems. On February 22, 1991, the US coalition begins its 100-hour ground war. Heavily armed US units drive deep into southern Iraq. Overall, 100,000 to 200,000 Iraqis are killed during the war.

1991 Shi'ites in the south and Kurds in the north rise up against Hussein's regime in Iraq. The United States, after encouraging these uprisings during the war, now fears turmoil and instability in the region and refuses to support the rebels. The US denies the rebels access to captured Iraqi weapons and allows Iraqi helicopters to attack them.

1991 Iraq withdraws from Kuwait and agrees to an UN-brokered cease-fire, but the US and Britain insist that devastating sanctions remain effective. The US declares large parts of north and south Iraq "no-fly" zones for Iraqi aircraft.

1991 US military deployments continue after the war, with 17,000 to 24,000 US troops in the Persian Gulf region at any given time [Christian Science Monitor].

1992 US Marines land near Mogadishu, Somalia, supposedly to ensure humanitarian relief and "restore order." But the US also plans to remove the dominant warlord, Mohammed Aidid, and install a more pro-US regime. In June 1993, after numerous gun battles with Aidid forces, US helicopters strafe Aidid supporters, killing scores. In October, when US forces attempt to kidnap two Aidid lieutenants, a fierce gun battle breaks out. Five US helicopters are shot down, 18 US soldiers killed and 73 wounded, while 500 to 1000 Somalians are killed and many more injured.

1992 The US Defense Department drafts new, post-Soviet "Defense Planning Guidance" paper stating, "In the Middle East and Southwest Asia, our overall objective is to remain the predominant outside power in the region and preserve US and Western access to the region's oil."

1993 The US brokers a "peace" agreement between Israel and the Palestine Liberation Organization at Oslo, Norway. The agreement strengthens Israel and US domination, while leaving Palestinians a small part of their historic homeland, broken up into isolated pieces surrounded by Israel. No provisions are made for the return of the four million Palestinian refugees living outside of Israel, the West Bank, and Gaza.

1993 The US launches missile attack on Iraq, claiming self-defence against an alleged assassination attempt on former president Bush two months earlier.

1995 The US imposes oil and trade sanctions against Iran, reinforcing sanctions in effect since 1979, for alleged sponsorship of 'terrorism', seeking to acquire nuclear arms, and hostility to the Middle East process.

1995 With US backing, Turkey launches a major military offensive, involving some 35,000 Turkish troops, against the Kurds in northern Iraq.

1998 Congress passes the "Iraq Liberation Act," giving nearly $100 million to groups attempting to overthrow the Hussein regime.

1998 Claiming retaliation for attacks on US embassies in Tanzania and Kenya, President Clinton sends 75 cruise missiles pounding into rural Afghanistan—supposedly targeting Osama Bin Laden. The US also destroys a factory producing half of Sudan's pharmaceutical supply, claiming the factory is involved in chemical warfare. The US later acknowledges there is no evidence for the chemical warfare charge.

1998 The US and Britain launch "Operation Desert Fox" in December. It is a bombing campaign supposedly aimed at destroying Iraq's nuclear, chemical and biological weapons programs. For most of the next year, US and British planes strike Iraq every day with missiles.

1999 The US Department of Defense shifts command of its forces in Central Asia from the Pacific Command to the Central Command, underlining the heightened importance of the region, which includes vast oil reserves in and around the Caspian Sea.

January 2001—Tenth anniversary of the US war on Iraq: sanctions still in place and the UN estimates that 4,500 children are dying per month from disease and malnutrition as a result. The US planes, which have flown over 280,000 sorties in Iraq over the past decade, continue to attack from the air.

CIA assassination initiatives [killinghope.org] to preserve or promote "liberty, sovereignty and world peace."

In the last leg of this chapter on chronology and timelines, the final passage is comparatively brief—it is a list of international leaders, statesmen, or other individuals whose attempted and sometimes successful assassinations the United States has been involved in since the end of World War II. This is adapted from William Blum's "CIA's Assassination Initiatives." In an attempt to track the Master of the World, this chapter might look like a library catalogue already; my apologies for that.

1949 Kim Koo, Korean opposition leader

1950s CIA/Neo-Nazi hit list of more than 200 political figures in West Germany to be "put out of the way" in the event of a Soviet invasion

1950s Zhou En Lai, Prime Minister of China, several attempts on his life

1957–62 Sukarno, President of Indonesia

1951 Kim II Sung, Premier of North Korea

1953 Mohammed Mossadegh, Prime Minister of Iran

1950s Claro M. Recto, Philippines opposition leader

1955 Jawaharlal Nehru, Prime Minister of India

1957 Gamal Abdul Nasser, President of Egypt

1959–60s Norodom Sihanouk, leader of Cambodia

1960 Brig. Gen. Abdul Karim Kassem, leader of Iraq

1950s–70s Jose Figueres, President of Costa Rica, two attempts on his life

1961 Francois "Papa Doc" Duvalier, leader of Haiti

1961 Patrice Lumumba, Prime Minister of the Congo

1961 Gen. Rafael Trujillo, leader of Dominican Republic

1963 Ngo Dinh Diem, President of South Vietnam

1960s Fidel Castro, President of Cuba, many attempts and plots on his life

1960s Raul Castro, high official in government of Cuba

1965 Francisco Caamano, Dominican Republic opposition leader

1965–6 Charles de Gaulle, President of France

1967 Che Guevara, Cuban leader

1970 Salvador Allende, President of Chile

1970 Gen. Rene Schneider, C—in—C of Army, Chile

1970s–81 General Omar Torrijos, leader of Panama

1972 General Manuel Noriega, Chief of Panama Intelligence

1975 Mobutu Sese Seko, President of Zaire

1976 Michael Manley, Prime Minister of Jamaica

1980–86 2011 onwards: Moammar Qaddafi, leader of Libya, several plots and attempts upon his life

1982 Ayatollah Khomeini, leader of Iran

1983 Gen. Ahmed Dlimi, Moroccan Army commander

1983 Miguel d'Escoto, Foreign Minister of Nicaragua

1984 The nine comandantes of the Sandinista National Directorate

1985 Sheikh Mohammed Hussein Fadlallah, Lebanese Shiite leader

1991 Saddam Hussein, leader of Iraq

1993 Mohamed Farah Aideed, prominent clan leader of Somalia

1998 Osama bin Laden, leading Islamic militant

2001–11 Osama bin Laden, leading Islamic militant

1999 Slobodan Milosevic, President of Yugoslavia

2002 Gulbuddin Hekmatyar, Afghan Islamic leader and warlord

2003 Saddam Hussein and his two sons

Mine eyes have seen the orgy of the launching of the Sword
He is searching out the hoardings where the strangers' wealth is
*   stored*
He hath loosed his fateful lightnings, and with woe and death
*   has scored.*
His lust is marching on.
       —Mark Twain, *The Battle Hymn of the Republic*

4 Demonizing Communism — *The 1st Protection Racket*

It was the cleverest protection racket since men convinced women that they needed men to protect them—if all the men vanished overnight, how many women would be afraid to walk the streets?

—William Blum

As Adam chewed the apple the wise men promptly pointed out that it was on Eve's insistence that the poor guy fell. Probably Adam was a senseless bloke with no opinion, who wanted to gnaw at something and was deceived in his innocence. Probably he was too smart and feigned virtuousness, knowing well that Eve was the only scapegoat within miles. We would never know. To make things worse for Eve, there was always a tacit acknowledgment of the fact that this act of eating the fruit was not good for humanity.

The US wanted to gnaw at something when it was gradually emerging as the world's largest industrial economy and bully. It wanted Latin America for rounding out its natural boundaries, and to protect its home turf. It wanted the industrial nerve-centre Germany, and Europe of course, to secure strategic depth. It also wanted the Middle East to strengthen its grip on world energy resources and supply. Three big apples. But there was no Eve to take the blame. The propaganda machine, which by then was getting huge, was commissioned to create one. The resultant spin that the American media created was that the United States, the only truly free country in the world, was insulating the world by preaching its message of liberty, open markets, 'way of life'—to pre-empt the threat of Communism and an imminent Soviet takeover. Eve was as clueless as ever, but this time around, Adam had smartened over the years. The so-called legitimacy of the exercise also overruled any questions of tacit or explicit acknowledgment of the amoral nature of it—if the USA wanted to chew, humanity could go to hell.

What was Eve's fault? When the Soviet Socialist Republic was being formed out of the Bolshevik Revolution during 1918, communism was envisaged as the only real threat to Western interests, and for real reasons. This was a form of governance that took into account the questions of the mass, something that went against the basic tenet of the Western imperial model. The Bolsheviks exhibited some radical pragmatism too. During this time they made a separate peace with Germany in order to get out of a war they regarded as imperialist and which did not concern them in any way. They also intended to try and rebuild a Russia that was war torn, devastated, tired, homeless, and hungry. And the ultimate nail in the coffin was that the "Bolsheviks had displayed the far greater audacity of overthrowing a capitalist- feudal system and proclaiming the first socialist state in the history of the world. This was uppity-ness writ incredibly large. This was the crime the Allies had to punish, the virus which had to be eradicated lest it spread to their own people" [Blum, *Killing Hope, Part 1*, 6].

The "Why" we all know by now; the greed based motives have been discussed at length already. The "How" opens up that phase in time that witnessed a newfound armament, unofficially called American Propaganda machinery, which was to finally complete the shape of greed dynamics—muffling serious concerns about the world, around the world. So, '[B]y the summer of 1918 some 13,000 American troops could be found in the newly-born Union of Soviet Socialist Republics" [Blum, *Killing Hope, Part 1*, 6]. This set of aggression extended to a country whose soldiers had recently fought alongside them for over three years and suffered more casualties than any other country on either side of the World War.

The Background

The United States had become the world's major industrial economy by early 1900. It was the leading creditor too. The Great Depression was largely contained through a successful intervention in World War II—an event that saw US industrial production jump over three times. And after the World War, having displaced Europe from the Western Hemisphere and "(W)ith much of the world in ruins, the US had attained a historically unparalleled peak of economic and military dominance. State and corporate planners were well aware of their unprecedented power, and intent on using it to construct a global order to benefit the interests they serve" [Chomsky, *Year 501*, 51]. An interesting lesson for the corporate managers of the US who managed the wartime economy was that there was no second way of maximising private wealth and power other than by large scale state intervention. The tag line must have been something like, "Want to nurture, sustain and enhance wealth? Call for government muscle." Closely coinciding in concept, though not so much in language, were the written words of Major General Smedley Butler, a decorated US war hero, in his book *War as a Racket'*. But since capitalism in theory is all about private enterprise, it remained the same workable system "only in rhetorical flourishes, or on the remote margins" [Chomsky, *Year 501*, 51].

There were several priorities. The details of the fate of Latin America have already been dealt with in the last chapter. After World War II, the importance of the traditional service role of the South was enhanced by "the realization that the food and fuel of Eastern Europe were no longer available to Western Europe at pre-war levels" (Leffler). Each region was assigned its status and "function" by the planners [Chomsky, *Year 501*, 54]. Number two was to ensure that the industrial core of Europe, Germany, and Japan remained within "US-dominated world power." It was achieved through a control mechanism by domestic financial-industrial sectors linked to US state-corporate power. With Germany, in the first leg, the Allies abolished the armed forces, the munitions factories and civilian industries that could support them. "This included the destruction of all ship and aircraft manufacturing capability"[wikipedia.org]. Then they proceeded to put serious operational restrictions on the "civilian industries which might have a military potential" [Smith, Jean Edward, *American Exploitation of Postwar Germany*, 135–142]. That resulted in a virtual clamp on the rest. Then the Allies stopped German trade in coal and steel in exchange for food from neighboring European nations like Turkey, Holland, and Denmark. The United States then confiscated large amounts of German intellectual property (patents, copyrights and trademarks). Beginning immediately after the German surrender and continuing for the next two years the

U.S. pursued a vigorous program to harvest all technological and scientific know-how as well as all patents in Germany. They included items and drawings etc. of the electron microscope, textile machinery, tape recorders, a chocolate-wrapping machine, a continuous butter-making machine, ice skate grinders "and other technologies—almost all of which were either new to American industry or 'far superior' to anything in use in the United States" [Smith, Jean Edward, *American Exploitation of Postwar Germany*, 135–142]. During the Cold War however, following a near-collapse of the German economy and fear of a resultant voluntary embrace of communism by the West German population, US policy makers decided that it was time to restore some financial and industrial colour by calling off the dismantling of industrial Germany and rebuilding it through a decentralised US state-corporate control mechanism.

A sub priority of the reconstruction of Europe was the exploitation of Africa. Southeast Asia was put aside for Japan (George Kennan and his State Department Policy Planning Staff, 1948-1949).

The Third and most crucial priority was to dent the anti-fascist resistance, to weaken labour, and to restore traditional conservative rule, often including fascist collaborators. That part was accomplished on a global scale starting from the late 40s, often violently as and when required. Readers have acquired a fair idea of this through the earlier chapter. Patterns remained the same, whether in Nicaragua or Korea or Greece. The fundamentals were kept simple. The interests of the US economy were number one. At number two was the question of direct or indirect control. Though the US liked to project that its world view was based on the principles of liberal internationalism, for all practical purposes it did quite the opposite because serious wealth and power interests always remained the principle stake. So, for example, to control the imperial system that Japan had sought to construct called for 'decisions to favour traditional colonial preference systems for rival/allies. . ..' And finally, the final question was whether to include the rest of the Allies in decision-making across certain places of the globe. For instance, US policy makers completely barred its allies from any role in determining the fate of Japan. "The goal was 'to guarantee U.S. security by insuring long-term American domination of Japan and to exclude the influence of all foreign governments. . ..' Given US power, that goal was easily attained, irrespective of wartime agreements" [Chomsky, *Year 501*, 52].

To find instances of the US successfully thwarting antifascist resistance, Italy serves as an accomplishment of classical nature, achieved through a mix of gentle persuasion, force, and a lot of propaganda. Like Greece, it was deemed important for extended control of the Middle East through the Mediterranean Sea. During 1948 there were some serious proportions of communist feeling among the voters in Italy, preceding the elections. The Communist Party had a strong labour support base, and it had a legacy of opposing fascism and the Nazi occupiers. It was popular; popular enough to win the elections. That result could have a "demoralizing effect throughout Western Europe, the Mediterranean, and the Middle East," US policymakers warned. It would be the "first instance in history of a communist accession to power by popular suffrage and legal procedure," and "so unprecedented and portentous an event must produce a profound psychological effect. . ." [Chomsky, *Year 501*, 52]. Practically, that kind of a result could prompt popular movements across other parts of US dominion, parts that sought to pursue an independent and democratic course. And that kind of a trend could seriously damage the US-designed world order of conservative and profascist dominated zones. So to prevent Italy from becoming a "virus infecting others," there were different levels of US interventions that remained active until the mid 1970s.

Chile, Nicaragua—we know the sequence by now—but what was unique in Italy's case was a novel attempt to mitigate the disruptive population, brought into effect by inducing mass emigration. A significant chunk of the Marshall Plan aid, which flowed into Italy at the end of World War II, was used to rebuild the Italian "merchant marine to 'double the number of Italian emigrants who can be carried overseas each year,' the chief of the ECA (Marshall Plan) mission for Italy reported." This win-win equation was a sure shot, since Europe had unemployment problems after 1945. Of course the US did not want any more Italian emigrants, so the "Congress. . .authorised funds for the 'purpose of transporting emigrants from Italy to parts of the world other than the United States.' " [Chomsky, *Year 501*, 52]. So it was South America (Brazil in 1950, specifically) and Europe where the labour supporters or prodemocracy voters were seen off to.

There were other large scale initiatives. Media propaganda was the most prominent mass-conditioning agent. For starters, there was a massive letter-writing campaign from Italian-Americans to their relatives and friends in Italy. It was said to be first written by individuals in their own words under the guidance of sample letters in newspapers. This ploy soon began to get "expanded to mass-produced, pre-written, postage-paid form letters, cablegrams, 'educational circulars,' and posters, needing only an address and signature." The handwritten scripts soon graduated to pictures and illustrations. The Committee to Aid Democracy in Italy started distributing "half a million picture postcards illustrating the gruesome fate awaiting Italy if it voted for 'dictatorship' or 'foreign dictatorship.' " it is today estimated that in all about ten million letters were "written and distributed by newspapers, radio stations, churches, the American Legion, wealthy individuals, etc.; and business advertisements now included offers to send letters airmail to Italy even if you didn't buy the product." The content of the letters was designed to play on the fears of the Italian public, outlining how a communist victory would surely ruin Italy because then the US would withdraw financial support. They also hinted at a possible third world war. Terming communism "cruel" and "despotic," the letters urged the citizens "not to throw" the country to them. Symbolic phrases, like "torch of liberty" and "forces of true democracy" that were sure to die if the communists came to power, were also used [Blum, *Killing Hope, Part 1*, 29].

There were less sophisticated messages too. Those letters narrated quite explicitly that if the US stopped sending money, then the letter writers would be compelled to do the same. Others warned about loss of religion and the church, loss of family life, and loss of home and land if there were Soviet domination of Italy. These were individual endeavours mostly. Representing official opinion were the US State Department and the 1953 Nobel Peace Prize winner George Marshall, who continued to repeat the "threats of cutting off aid" [Blum, *Killing Hope, Part 1*, 29].

Then there was the radio. A daily series of direct broadcasts to Italy backed by the State Department featuring key Americans was introduced. These messages were expected to reach 1.2 million people in Italy in 1946. The airwaves were constantly filled with rhetoric. Italians were subjected to vivid pictures of their future life, which boiled down to a "choice between democracy and communism, between God and god-lessness, between order and chaos." There were warnings—some pretty naïve. Speakers went to lengths to describe how "under a communist dic-tatorship in Italy," many of the "nation's industrial plants would be dis-mantled and shipped to Russia and millions of Italy's workers would be deported to Russia for forced labour." To drive home the fact, "a parade of unknown but passionate refugees from Eastern Europe went before the microphone to recount horror stories of life behind 'The Iron Cur-tain.' " Over time, as the elections drew closer, Voice of America's daily broadcasts into Italy increased. At one end, there were show-biz greats like Frank Sinatra and Gary Cooper, at the other end there were regu-lar Italian-American housewives—all were brought in to broadcast their views to influence Italians. In the middle of the spectrum, unbelievably, the "Italian-American Labour leader Luigi Antonini called upon Italians to "smash the Muscovite fifth column,' the followers of the 'ferocious Moscow tyranny,' to prevent Italy from becoming an 'enemy totalitarian country' " [Blum, *Killing Hope, Part 1*, 29].

There were several other well-synchronised initiatives. From movies that Hollywood produced (Ninotchka, which lampooned Soviet life), ex-hibitions, accusations that the Soviet Union plotted the subjugation of Western Europe, serving notice that Italians who joined the Communists would be denied emigration to America, signing a ten-year treaty with Italy, introducing a "Friendship Train" to tour America collecting gifts for Italians, to a "Manifesto of peace to freedom-loving Italians," that cir-culated in Italian newspapers. The American Labour Council contributed $50,000 to anti-Communist labour organizations in Italy. The CIA, by its own later admission, gave $1 million to Italian "centre parties", a king's ransom in Italy in 1948. Then President Truman, in a sudden display of magnanimity just one month before the election, transferred twenty-nine merchant ships to the Italian government; Italian vessels that were seized during the war [Blum, *Killing Hope, Part 1*, 29].

Then there was last minute aid. The House Appropriations Commit-tee approved $18.7 million in interim aid. A few weeks later, the United States gave another $4.3 million. Then, six days before the election the "State Department made it public that Italy would soon receive $31 mil-lion in gold in return for gold looted by the Nazis. (The fact that only a few years earlier Italy had been the 'enemy' fighting alongside the Nazis was now but a dim memory)" [Blum, *Killing Hope, Part 1*, 30]. Barely 48 hours after that, the US government authorised two further large shipments of food to Italy, each one for $8 million worth of grains. With these, every effort was made to make the Italians realise how Americans were saving them from starvation.

* * * *

Historically in the Third World there has been an effort towards self-determination, specifically a need to pursue a path of development that is independent of the United States. "This has been manifested in (a) the ambition to free themselves from economic and political subservience to the United States; (b) the refusal to minimise relations with the socialist bloc, or suppress the left at home, or welcome an American military installation on their soil; in short, a refusal to be a pawn in the Cold War; or (c) the attempt to alter or replace a government which held to neither of these aspirations; i.e., a government supported by the United States" [Blum, *Killing Hope, Part 1*, 11]. The case, contrary to whatever the United States government and its propaganda machine had to say, has not been about communist takeover, ever. But time and again we have seen that countries have been subjected to terrorist attacks, invasions, and/or unparalleled economic embargoes and subversion. In 1918, the American capitalists needed no reasons to fight the communists. The Soviets were going through an all time low in terms of devastation of property, their economy, and human lives, and were painstakingly rebuilding their nation then. Indoctrinating the rest of the world with Bolshevism featured nowhere in their plan of things. But the American barons did what they did because fundamentally communism was perceived as a threat to their wealth and privilege, "although their opposition was expressed in terms of moral indignation" [Blum, *Killing Hope, Part 1*, 9]. We know a fair amount about the US gunboat diplomacy that operated as a result in the Caribbean, to ensure the fortunes of United Fruit and W.R. Grace & Co. while there was a legitimate recognition of the fact that the "Russians were not responsible for the conflicts in the Third World (Dean Acheson 1952)" [Chomsky, *Year 501*, 57].

There was one more fear in the minds of the barons of the US capitalist system, on a par with communism: the "neutrality" of nations. Neutralism was a "shortcut to suicide" as Secretary of State Dean Acheson had noted [americaversuseurope.com]. There were explicit warnings to European nations about the perils of neutrality. Take the example of Germany. The creation of NATO was in part motivated by communism and in part motivated by the fear of neutrality; the intent was to "integrate Western Europe and England into an orbit amenable to American leadership," for it was considered absolutely vital that "Neither an integrated Europe nor a united Germany nor an independent Japan (should) be permitted to emerge as a third force or a neutral bloc" [Leffler, *A Preponderance of Power*, 17].

For all practical purposes Western planners "did not expect and were not worried about Soviet aggression." On the contrary, they were worried that "the Soviets might really be interested in striking a deal, unifying Germany, and ending the division of Europe." This was a direct opposition, a threat to American hegemonic interests, for, a unified Germany with a possible tilt towards neutralism was, going by Acheson, a shortcut to suicide [Leffler, *A Preponderance of Power*, 282–283].

" 'The real issue,' the CIA concluded in 1949, 'is not the settlement of Germany,' which, it was believed—and feared—might be reached by an accord with the Kremlin. Rather, it is 'the long-term control of German power.' This 'great workshop' must be controlled by the US and its clients, with no participation from the Soviet Union, despite the well-understood security interests of the country that had just been virtually destroyed by Germany for the second time in 30 years. . .." What was clearly more important to the United States was, a) weakening of the Soviet Union and b) maintaining their dominance over Europe. "Division of Germany was therefore to be preferred, with the Soviet Union excluded from any voice over the heartland of German industry in the wealthy Ruhr/Rhine industrial complex" [Chomsky, *Year 501*, 57–58].

So it was certainly not the fear of Bolshevik influence on the rest of the world throwing a spanner into the greed-system of USA—because clearly, the Soviets were never up to the challenge. On the contrary, the little initiatives that they took or views that they expressed actually underlined their intention to reducing tension, at least in the European sphere. One could not blame them for that—they were the ones that took the maximum brunt of the two World Wars. But as I have argued earlier, if Eve was not there, she had to be manufactured. If she was there somewhere, but did not have the required mental constitution, that had to be created too. Americans after all are well known for their entrepreneurial abilities. The Western media therefore spent a good chunk of their productive time throughout the 20th century giving to the world a scapegoat called "communism."

The Propaganda

Thus, communists, unlike normal human beings, did not take jobs in the government—they "infiltrated" it. Communists did not support a particular program—they "exploited" it. Communists did not back Arbenz—they "used" him. Moreover, communists "controlled" the labour movement and land reform. . ." 'The basic idea behind the employment of such language—which was standard Western fare throughout the Cold War — was to deny the idea that communists could be people sincerely concerned about social change. American officials denied it to each other as well as to the world' [Blum, *Killing Hope, Part 1*, 73].

The anti-communist propaganda campaign started before 1918 ended. The First World War was not over then. Allied forces were fighting alongside Russia, against Germany. But that did not prevent headlines like "Red Peril", "the Bolshevik assault on civilization", and "menace to world by Reds is seen" to become staple dosage for public through the New York Times. This trend continued. 1919 and 20 saw New York Times coming out with more such headlines. Banners like "Reds Seek War With America" or "Reds Raising Army To Attack India" or "Allied officials and diplomats [envisage] a possible invasion of Europe" were all too common throughout these years [Blum, *Killing Hope, Part 1*, 7]. This set of news intended to drive a belief that a nation that was shattered through a devastating war, a nation in turmoil due to a revolution and near dead fighting a foreign-force sponsored civil war— was actually planning to invade other states. Amazingly the propaganda actually succeeded!

Success was largely a matter of numbers—that of reaching the maximum number of people. Success was also a matter of continuous assault to logic and reason. 'From the Red Scare of the 1920s to the Mc-Carthyism of the 1950s to the Reagan Crusade against the Evil Empire of the 1980s, the American people have been subjected to a relentless anti-communist indoctrination.' As a result, by 1945 when the Second World War was finally over, and the first wave of anti-communist propaganda was gradually making way for a second one, "every American past the age of 40 had been subjected to some 25 years of anti-communist radiation, the average incubation period needed to produce a malignancy. Anti-communism had developed a life of its own, independent of its capitalist father" [Blum, *Killing Hope, Part 1*, 9]. True. But it was not just restricted only within the United States of America. The propagandist's well charted plan that was to span over a period of more than 40-50 years, would soon produce an incredible number of people across the globe that were averse to anything that was even remotely related to the words Marxism or communism.

'The inimitable' PG Wodehouse, once expressing his views about drinking, wrote ". . .it starts with a faint pleasure, and ends in an obsession". Eventually during the post war period, as a chunk of the incredibly large mass of middle aged anti-communist American population found way into the realms of governance and policy-making—the propaganda hit home. It became intrinsic, constitutional to the psyche of both American domestic and foreign policy, as these diplomats saw the world out there as one composed of "communists" and "anti-communists", whether of nations, movements or individuals. John Foster Dulles simplified it by saying "For us there are two sorts of people in the world: there are those who are Christians and support free enterprise and there are the others". A "us and them" - an involuntary reflex, where "us" represented the so-called innocent, freedom loving Americans, and "them" could be anyone, 'a peasant in the Philippines, a mural-painter in Nicaragua, a legally-elected prime minister in British Guiana, or a European intellectual, a Cambodian neutralist, an African nationalist — all, somehow, part of the same monolithic conspiracy; each, in some way, a threat to the American Way of Life. . . the "communist threat"' [Blum, *Killing Hope, Part 1*, 10]. What had started a few years ago as a propaganda tool to pre-empt a probable threat to the Greed System had gradually become a moral imperative — an obsession. One of the most well known current-day products of such obsession being an American President himself, who, with all his faculties, believed in "Either you are with us, or you are with the terrorists"[yc2.net].

Sadly enough, these assumptions and arguments were never questioned. One question that writer William Blum puts forward is "why would the Soviets want to invade Western Europe or bomb the United States? They clearly had nothing to gain by such actions except the almost certain destruction of their country, which they were painstakingly rebuilding once again after the devastation of the war." A relevant second question is, assuming all reports of mainstream media to be true, how was it always so easy for the Soviets to incite a set of people into "uprising" or 'invasion" or whatever other actions described? US government and the CIA tried to spark mass revolt in China, Cuba, the Soviet Union, Albania, and elsewhere in Eastern Europe with a singular lack of success. They had all the money, muscle, media and strategic partners that one could possibly think of and yet they failed an incredible number of times. In fact the US has never managed to initiate a popular revolution. So how could a tattered nation with impoverished people and a near defunct infrastructure consummate such stuffs like "assault" or "infiltration", so lucidly articulated?

No one questioned. No one answered. The resultant US military budget ran up to $300 billion by the 1980s, and the moral imperative of post-war Americans ran from strength to strength as their anti-communist manifesto found a place in comic books, school books, newspapers, magazines, stand-up comedy shows, Hollywood movies, and ministers' sermons. The resultant conviction fashioned by this assault upon the intellect produced a sinister mix of people—they were the result of the greed-system, but they had no idea about it. Their obsession with their way of life needed no reason, no motivation. A frenzied mob, super-saturated with consumerist and exploitative views of the world and life, and justified in their race for salvation through the American Way of Life—the same way of life that would transcend into universal aspiration soon after the fall of the Berlin Wall.

Eve was manufactured, manipulated, and in course of time destroyed. And from the aegis of this process came out billions of people, representative of a psyche bereft of most of the constructive aspects of individual/social intellectual growth or appreciation, vision or mission.

Out came a new world of people loyal to their creator—the Greed System.

5 Of Globalisation — *The Greedster Effect on Commerce*

Given the stakes involved, it is hardly surprising that politics has once again become the servant of economics.

—P.S. Jha, *Twilight of the Nation State: Globalisation, Chaos and War*

Many of us who grew up in India during the eighties, seventies, sixties, or slightly before missed out on quite a few tangibles in life, those that a present day kid cannot even think of being without. Putting aside the big-time revolutions like the internet or wireless mobile connectivity, even small things like a bottle of Coca Cola were coveted objects to us. It was not that all of us were poor financially—we just had no access. I come from a town called Durgapur that had one functional movie hall and zero restaurants till the late 80s. And of course the entire country had just one TV channel—the Doordarshan.

During the 90s however, things started changing. The soft-socialist status made way for a more open policy in national economy and trade, there were rapid strides towards (consumerist) modernization—most of us have witnessed or are aware of it. The key change in India's policy was fiscal. And the results have been unprecedented. While we overcame the liquidity crisis, we also quickly managed to push the backbone of the traditional Indian economy—agriculture—toward oblivion.

Important as it is, and even though this will be picked up at a later stage as part of a broader debate, vanishing agriculture is not the key point in discussion right now. During the 90s India was getting formally indoctrinated into the process of globalisation, a mechanism that has been around for quite some time. "Globalization" is defined as "the acceleration and intensification of interaction and integration among the people, companies, and governments of different nations. This process has effects on human well-being (including health and personal safety),

81

on the environment, on culture (including ideas, religion, and political systems), and on economic development and prosperity of societies across the world" [globaled.org]. Well, theoretically. Practically, this apparently well-meaning, decent-looking, Samaritan, humanitarian course of global goodwill, according to Brazilian journalist, writer, and sociopolitical observer Pepe Escobar, is "...like Poe's maelstrom. A black void, rather. No one can escape it. And we don't know how it ends" [Escobar, *Globalistan*, 15]. Globaled.org puts the practical version of globalisation as "Americanization of world culture and United States dominance of world affairs...a force for environmental devastation, exploitation of the developing world, and suppression of human rights" [globaled.org (pdf)].

So why these two extremely polarised versions when practice is pitched against theory? To try and understand that, we need to look a little deeper, even travel a little back in time.

Taking Stock of the Medieval Trade Control Mechanism
Dr. J.W. Smith, founder of the Institute for Economic Democracy, has a great deal to tell us about this question in his books and blog to be found at ied.info:

> During the middle ages European commerce and industry was town-centered and controlled. The grip was such that the expertise was not even allowed to get out into the open country. Technology was essentially controlled to maintain access to resources, to maintain superiority in terms of wealth-producing processes. This was the basis of Europe's self-learning to plunder by trade. But that is not to say that the rural centers would fall behind and dwindle almost immediately. They would, more often than not, put up a fight. For instance, the struggle between the urban centers against rural trading and rural handicrafts lasted at least seven or eight hundred years. The severity of these measures increased with the growth of "democratic government" [ied.info].

Why would the struggle take place in the first place? Was it chiefly competition or was there some added element too?

Primitive industrial capital was simple. Looms and fulling vats were the key armaments of the urban cloths' guild. With these, the cities could produce cheaper and better cloth and trade these commodities to the countryside for wool and food. J.W. Smith, in his book *The World's Wasted Wealth 2*, writes that "when the serfs came to town and looked at the simple looms and fulling vats, it did not take them long to build their own tools and produce their own cloth" [worldproutassembly.org]. That was catastrophic for the urban merchants. The resulting loss of the urban centers due to this sudden increased knowledge base of the rural industry meant "impoverishment and possibly even starvation" for those in the city who formerly produced that cloth [ied.info]. The same loss of monopoly registered across other mechanisms of urban business too, which was the result of an increased technological knowledge-base of the countryside. In short, the farmers did not need to buy from the towns— they were capable of their own manufacture. This was a stumbling block. The wealth-producing process had to be protected. The comparative advantages of the outlying villages had to be eliminated. Dependence upon the city had to be maintained, and the raw material of the rural geography as well as the finished product had to be city-controlled. The only option available was brute force. So, throughout "the fourteenth century regular armed expeditions were sent out against all the villages in the neighborhood and looms and fulling-vats were broken or carried away" [ied.info].

The problem of the towns collectively was to control their own markets, that is, be able to reduce the cost of items purchased from the countryside and to minimise the role of outside merchants. Two techniques were used. On the one hand, towns sought to obtain not only legal rights to tax market operations but also the right to regulate the trading operation (who should trade, when it should take place, what should be traded). Furthermore, they sought to restrict the possibilities of their countryside engaging in trade other than *via* their town. Over time, these various mechanisms shifted their terms of trade in favor of the townsmen, in favor thus of the urban commercial classes against both the landowning and peasant classes [ied.info].

* * *

While religion and political ideologies remained as the two prominent reasons for global conflicts, the economy was destined to overtake them as the most crucial factor—witnessed right from the time isolated trade and commercial relations were established (often forced) on different communities. Smith rightly argues that one of the key reasons behind the wars between the city-states of the Middle Ages was control of trade. Eventually the victorious city-states would evolve into countries, seeking more control of trade through more wars, and finally evolve into empires, controlling resources and trade far beyond their own borders.

Zygmunt Bauman's Liquid Modernity

Human transitions have always had deeper meanings, from natural forces, to initial control through trade, to geography, colonisation, weapons, and fear, making way for a Greed System in a new world order. Polish philosopher Zygmunt Bauman has a wonderful way of enlightening us through his epic book *Liquid Modernity*. For those who do not have the energy, resources, or inclination to pick up and study Bauman's work in detail, we can take a small tour through that fraction of his concepts which are particularly relevant here.

Bauman has established that modernity as a concept starts when space and time are separated from living practice and from each other and so become ready to be theorised as distinct and mutually independent categories of strategy and action. "...In the modern struggle between time and space, space was the solid and stolid, unwieldy and inert side, capable of waging only a defensive, trench war—being an obstacle to the resilient advances of time. Time was the active and dynamic side in the battle, the side always on the offensive: the invading, conquering and colonizing force" [Bauman, *Liquid Modernity*].

Solid *vs* Liquid

He proceeds to take up solids to explain liquids. The term 'solid' is used chiefly as a metaphor for medieval or pre-modern institutions and establishments that were bound by certain old-school values, while 'liquid' denotes modernity. What primarily differentiates solids from liquids? Stability, achieved through the concept of bonding. Bonding allows solids to put up a resistance 'against separation of the atoms.' As a result, solids cancel time; they are compact, built to last and can withstand weathering. From concept to practice, examples of units that correlate with solids could be a society, a factory, a family, or a classroom. They are old and have been around for some time—thus they exhibit stability through bonding.

Liquids however are completely time-bound. Just as when describing solids one may ignore time altogether—you know, the likes of parent-children relation or marriage—something that has been on for hundreds of years, to leave time out of account while describing fluids, Bauman writes, would be a grievous mistake. Descriptions of fluids are all snapshots, because they are continuously changing shapes, ever-flowing. They need a date at the bottom of the picture.

Liquids have several qualifying characteristics. They 'flow', 'spill', 'run out', 'splash', 'pour over', 'leak', 'flood', 'spray', 'drip', 'seep', 'ooze'—in short they are not easily stopped, unlike solids. In their motion they pass around some obstacles, dissolve some others and bore or soak their way through still others. Bauman notes that from their meeting with solids they emerge unscathed, while the solids they have met, if they stay solid, are changed - get moist or drenched. At times, there are chemical alterations in addition to the physical ones. And although it may not always be so, this extraordinary mobility of fluids is what associates them with the idea of 'lightness'. "We associate 'lightness' or 'weightlessness' with mobility and inconstancy; we know from practice that the lighter we travel the easier and faster we move" [Bauman, *Liquid Modernity*, 2–15].

Shaking Up the Wrong Things
Such a liquid is modern times. It has left a crucial impact on all the "solids" that have been described in the previous paragraphs. It did not look favourably upon the pre-modern solids and there was an urge to melt them. Whether the motive behind this wish was to discover or invent solids of "lasting solidity" for a more predictable and manageable world is debatable. Newcomers always tend to change the rules. The new government and the new boss always tends to "shake things up"—for various reasons or for want of one. Modern times, being the newcomer, was no different. Therefore, the first solids to be melted and the first ones to be profaned were "traditional loyalties, customary rights and obligations which bound. . . the enterprise." The mistake was the same that governments or bosses commit even today when in their overhauling

frenzy they forget that they might not have a reason at all. For building a new order seriously, there was this necessity to "get rid of the ballast with which the old order burdened the builders." That actually called for shredding the mostly nonsensical obligations "standing in the way of rational calculation of effects; as Max Weber put it, liberating business enterprise from the shackles of the family-household duties and from the dense tissue of ethical obligations." But that was not to happen. What happened actually left the whole complex society bare and unprotected, completely unarmed and impotent to "resist the business-inspired rules of action and business-shaped criteria of rationality, let alone to compete with them effectively." And this departure laid the field open to invasion and domination of Instrumental Rationality (Max Weber) or determining role of economy (Karl Marx). Bauman notes that this first melting of solids led to the progressive untying of the economy from its traditional political, ethical, and cultural entanglements [Bauman, *Liquid Modernity*, 4]. The first melting neutered ideologies; economics was to rule the future.

From Macro to Micro

So much for the new order. But modernity did not stop there. It is difficult to stop liquids. It gradually made an entry into the micro-levels of society. Earlier families were rock-solid structures. Although the Corleone's family values (minus the aura of criminality) during the time of Vito Corleone is something of an ideal illustration, there were many scaled-down versions of it in the world; you know people who considered their family to be the most important, the cardinal, the most sacrosanct entity in their lives. These days we have the parents and the children, but parenthood is disintegrating with a rise in the rates of divorce. The offspring are leading their own lives later in life, often away from their parents, and the grandparents are "included and excluded without any means of participating in the decisions of their sons and daughters" in a marked deviation from earlier times [Bauman, *Liquid Modernity*, 6].

In effect, the liquid modernity has altered the pre-modern solids radically. Since it is perpetually on the move, it has descended to "micro" levels of "social cohabitation." The liquids seep in, they change drastically and they keep changing, since keeping fluids in shape is difficult.

As a result of this extreme instability, the responsibility of success or failure is purely individual in nature. We can easily say that we now live in an individualised, privatised version of modernity—where each individual's fate depends on his or her ability to foresee or predict life and the future.

Global Capital Economy

The key components of globalisation are modernization—this is a relatively modern concept, liquid speed and flexibility—for rapid and smooth integration. Capitalist economics is the backbone of it, and the idea that drives it is our old friend greed, greed for power and wealth. Isolating each one of these components and examining them is necessary because at least the foreseeable future looks pretty much within this concept's grip. Having had a quick look at liquid modernity and the effects of it through the eyes of Bauman, let us see how capitalism takes a cue from the lightness, liquidity, and flexibility of modern times.

German scholar Horst Kurnitzky tells us that globalisation has configured "a new world, in which wealth and poverty, with no control by markets or the flux of cash, coexist with no form of social equality" [Escobar, *Globalistan*, 15]. Global capital economy, the new world order, or whatever you may choose to call it had originated from western Europe, and as "plunder by trade," as J.W. Smith termed it, came into vogue it took over the world—through colonization or otherwise.

Capitalism has its highs and lows. Some theorists, like Nikolai Kondratiev, called it cyclical waves that can be represented through crests or troughs, or oscillations, while philosophers like Trotsky preferred to see it as phases of establishment, breakage, or re-establishment of equilibrium [*Theory of Long Waves*, 1922]. A more recent observer, Pepe Escobar, sees capitalism as a "wrecker's ball" that smashes through equilibrium to produce anarchy, crises, and wars. Two inferences stand out in this among these conceptualizations. One is that this system produces extremes in excess—from polarised wealth to global chaos. The great depression of the 1930s, the subsequent World Wars, the post World War II expansion of the world economy, the 1970s recession and another in 2008 tell us exactly that. They also tell us another thing: the system is unpredictable. There is no "invisible hand". Modern capitalism is a stand-alone system. It is a by-product of a greed mechanism, far removed from its initial guiding philosophy, and it has a mind of its own.

This system transitioned through liquid modernity and now wants to be free flowing. For that to happen the world must be free of fences, barriers, fortified borders, and checkpoints. For a modernised capital economy, the network of social bonds, territories, institutions, states, and political or ideological affiliations are all obstacles that need to be cleared. In fact, there has been quite a lot of dismantling happening all over the world. There is a rough shape to it, and while this shape is quite wobbly it has a relatively fixed core.

Rules of Engagement

Power, a chief goal of the greed mechanism, has undergone radical changes. We find a little bit of Bauman here too. He explains how Michel Foucault used Jeremy Bentham's design of Panopticon as the most appropriate workable model to comprehend the applied mechanics of modern power. "In Panopticon the inmates were tied to the place and barred from all movement, confined within thick, dense, and closely guarded walls and fixed to their beds, cells, or work-benches." They were under watch. The watchers had relative mobility. The key was to control mobility over time. "The surveillants' " facility and expediency of movement was the warrant of their domination; the inmates' "fixedness to the place was. . .their subordination." Mastery over time was the secret. And freezing mobility was the principal strategy in their exercise of power. The pyramid was built on the basis of least mobility traveling upwards to highest mobility. The key components of the pyramid were velocity, access to the means of transportation, and the resulting freedom of movement. In other words, workers at the base were immobile. Their managers' degree of mobility depended on their place in the hierarchy [Bauman, *Liquid Modernity*, 9–10].

Let us take up a famous example from Bauman's book. Henry Ford decided one day to "double" the wages of his workers. The (publicly) declared reason was the celebrated phrase "I want my workers to be paid well enough to buy my cars." This was, obviously, a jest. The workers' purchases formed a derisory fraction of his sales, but their wages made a much greater part of his costs. The genuine reason to raise the wages was the formidable turnover of labour force with which Ford was confronted. He decided to give the workers a spectacular raise in order to fix them to the chain. The invisible chain riveting the workers to their working places and arresting their mobility was, in Cohen's words, "the heart of Fordism" [Bauman, *Liquid Modernity*, 58].

Panopticon was an expensive model. It needed space, constructions, administrations, cameras probably, residents' upkeep, equipment maintenance, the hiring of professionals, monitoring working conditions, and a whole lot of other things—in short, responsibility. Liquid modernity, as we have understood before, does not like the word. Responsibility binds, and is antagonistic to the very nature of liquid.

So welcome to the time of the Sinopticon, of drone wars, live-in relationships, and virtual friendships. If Panopticon engagements were based on an assumption that the people in control were "there somewhere," mostly nearby, now the people operating the levers of kinetics are either nowhere near or can disappear anytime. Either way they are as good as non-existent, at best, or undependable at worst—our version of the absentee landlord. "The end of Panopticon augurs the end of the era of mutual engagement: between the supervisors and the supervised, capital and labour, leaders and their followers, armies at war" [Bauman, *Liquid Modernity*, 11]. Rules of engagement now avoid territorial confinement, order-building, or taking responsibility for the consequences. The drones and the stealth bombers use "smart" self-guided missiles; they have replaced territorial infantry's whole endeavour of taking over a land. The unmarried couple no longer have to be bound by commitments; and the virtual friend no longer needs to lend a physical shoulder. Each of these can disappear/break-up/logout at anytime.

Liquid modernity in all its candour has touched another interesting human brainchild too: religious fundamentalism. From a handful of centralised, shoddily organised, highly ideological groups of the mid-20th century to individual fidayeens of the 21st century, with a personalised agenda, a hint of an ideological affiliation, the default Kalashnikov, and plenty of loose cash, the Islamic fundamentalism of modern times exhibits a remarkable departure from, say, the Islamic Brotherhood of 1928.

Neither Here Nor There

It is a kind of full circle. While modernising, there was this consistent and systematic assault of the settled, those converted to the sedentary way of life, against nomadic peoples and the nomadic style of life (Jim McLaughlin). The nomads were made the main villains in the way of progress and civilization. Modern "chronopolitics" posited them not just as inferior and primitive beings, underdeveloped and in need of reform and enlightenment, but also as backward and suffering from "cultural lag," lingering at the lower rungs of the evolutionary ladder, and unforgivably slow or morbidly reluctant to climb it, to follow the "universal pattern of development." Well, that chicken has come home to roost. In a most unusual revenge-of-nomadism, the settled majority is now "ruled by the nomadic and exterritorial elite. Keeping the roads free for nomadic traffic and phasing out the remaining check-points has now become the meta-purpose of politics, and also of wars. . ." [Bauman, *Liquid Modernity*, 12–13].

That brings us to a rather disturbing series of thoughts: The operating logic of modern times is, why hold the ground when it can be reached or abandoned at whim? Commitment can be an obstacle to exploiting new chances elsewhere. "Rockefeller might have wished to make his factories, railroads, and oil rigs big and bulky and own them for a long time. . . Bill Gates, however, feels no regret when parting with possessions in which he took pride yesterday; it is the mind-boggling speed of circulation, of recycling, aging, dumping and replacement which brings profit today—not the durability and lasting reliability of the product" [Bauman, *Liquid Modernity*, 13–14]. Heavy solid capital, fixed to the ground much like the labourers it engaged, has been dismantled by the light, liquid concept of modernity, where capital travels light—"with cabin luggage only, which includes no more than a briefcase, a cellular telephone and a portable computer." While poor labour "remains as immobilised as it was in the past—but the place which it once anticipated being fixed to once and for all has lost its past solidity. . ." [Bauman, *Liquid Modernity*, 58].

Resultant Globalization

Let us try to simplify things a bit. For starters, the modern world has given rise to a business class that does not want to have anything to do with responsibility. Greed has remained, but the earlier industrialists and rich men had a behavioural inviolable, that they took care of people or institutions that worked for (and with) them. The key to sustenance used to be in the consolidation of such resources. Not anymore. "Fordism" is dead and gone. What do we have now? We have the transnational corporations, or TNCs. These are corporations that operate in more than one country or nation at a time. Many of these companies have far more power than the nation-states across whose borders they operate, and are richer than those nations as well. They have absolutely no respect for the primaries like Labour or Environment. They are viral in nature. They operate as long as the variables are conducive, and move out whenever they so wish, leaving the host nation poor, jobless, and at times ecologically ravaged. Dr J.W. Smith puts it across this way: The primary cause of poverty in the middle of plenty has been uncovered. The sheriff and the courts are now enforcing the very same unequal property rights the cunning figured out 10,000 years ago.

As is covered in greater detail hereafter, fifty-one of the largest one hundred economies in the world are corporations and not nations. So where are these corporations based? France, Germany, the Netherlands, Japan, and the United States house 90% of the big TNCs. These corporations account for the modern world's industrial capacity, technological knowledge, financial transactions, and control. They mine nearly all of the gas and oil, build most of the power plants, dig up most of the minerals, sell most of the cars, planes, satellites, computers, chemicals, medicines—it is quite a list. They are growing or processing or distributing nearly all that you or I eat. They are also polluting the world irreversibly. [halexandria.org]

So how are they controlling overseas resources and ensuring the ease of their money making? After all the capitalist system is only an economic system, a mode of profit making, and not a legal, political, or military system. This is possible because they are blessed with something called the "Washington Consensus." This is the name for the new strategy of international financial capital that is dominant in the current system of capitalism (Nasser Zarafshan), which is driven by big capitalists' interests and managed through such apparatuses as the Federal Reserve, the International Monetary Fund, the World Bank, and the World Trade Organization. Of course there is tension between international capital's needs to keep profit rates high and sovereign nations that have different kinds of markets, resources, and workforces. That is precisely where all these institutions step in to ensure that capital travels light and free, without demarcations and borders and responsibilities. What do they do? They bring "economic pressure", says Nasser. Bodies like the IMF, the World Bank, and the WTO that have made a career out of putting economic pressure on various countries make these last bastions of the pre-liquid world conform to their neo-liberal strategy. They call it Structural Adjustment Programs. When this fails there can be resort to political and military pressures, and interventions [Zarafshan, *The Third Side also Exists*, www.mrzine.monthlyreview.org].

Neo-liberalism does not work for ordinary people and neither does removing the trade obstacles increase national incomes. There are literally scores of tests and surveys to confirm this. (Nasser has some really good results included in his article in mrzine.monthlyreview.org). At best, it creates more poverty and inequality. It also creates instability. Nations and regions that had adopted the neo-liberal strategy more thoroughly than others incurred heavier damage. Mexico in 1994–95, East Asia in 1997–98, Russia in 1998, and Argentina in 2001 are pretty good examples. John Weeks, in his article "Globalize, Globa-lize, Global Lies: Myths of the World Economy in the 1990s," based on the findings of similar research, states that "the country groups that introduced the globalisation policies to the greatest degree fared least well in the 1990s relative to previous decades (the OECD, the Latin American and the sub-Saharan countries); the best performing group since 1960, East and South-East Asia, entered into a severe recession in the 1990s; and the group whose growth improved in the 1990s without recession, South Asia, was that which least adopted policies of deregulation, trade liberalization and decontrol of the capital account." From the more solid productive capital, it is time for a more liquid financial capital these days. Using new financial instruments and innovative methods, revenues of financial capital have soared in the last two decades, in the most "fraudulent and parasitical fashion that has ever been witnessed in economic history." Its activities are different from production and trade—special efforts are taken to constitute an open space for dishonest, speculative financial manoeuvres. Enron Energy even made innovation of future weather and turned it into a means of profit-making. We all of course know the fate of the 70-billion dollar giant that, at its prime, bribed 212 out of 248 members of the U.S. Congress [Weeks, *Globalize, Globa-lize, Global Lies: Myths of the World Economy in the 1990s*]. Most major banks and corporations copied Enron's fictitious investment/production strategies. But they learned a lesson from Enron: when their racket crashed, just like Enron's did, they bailed themselves out as they controlled the Federal Reserve, while the rest of the country took the loss and paid the bill. Today these banks and financial institutions are earning more money investing in derivatives and other scams than ever before.

Capitalism is not a legal, political, or military system, theoretically. But under its influence the current picture looks somewhat like this: At the tip is the Triad—the US, EU, and Japan (with Israel, South Korea, Taiwan and Australia as sidekicks)—the greatest beneficiaries of the modern liquid global capital economy. There is a hint of a struggle between them, but we can overlook that as of now. They are the core. Between them and the rest of the world there lies a great imbalance. The Triad controls no less than 70% of the wealth of the planet. Of course poor Africa is at the far other end of the scale. Triad countries do all the research and development, with less than 1% of patents originating from outside their fraternity. Odd hubs like Bangalore only stress the template. There are 3 billion people barely surviving on less than $2 a day, 5 of the world's 6 billion people live on only 20% of the global GDP, while Hong Kong-Taipei, followed by New York-London remain the busiest air routes with global air passengers shooting up to 2 billion since 2005. The top 57% of the largest 500 organizations have no plans to fight global warming and 140 companies do not even bother to answer questions raised by the Carbon Disclosure Project [Escobar, *Globalistan*, 22–24

This is a topic that I have yet to explore in this discussion: environment degradation. From Gulf of Mexico oil spills to the burning of oil fields in Kuwait, the greed for wealth has seen unparalleled damage to the living conditions of our world. Since the examples are so numerous, and other people are writing books on it, here is just a single coin from a small pocket. I leave the rest to your enterprise.

The Niger Delta is home to the Ogoni people, but also to Africa's largest oil and gas industry, as developed by large TNCs such as Shell. The Nigerian government makes approximately $42 billion annually from its resources. They do not pass even a fraction of that to the locals. The unemployment rate in Ogoniland is around 90%. From 1976 to 1991 oil spills numbered around 3,000 at an average of 600 barrels per spill. Gas flaring, a practice widely recognised as the cause of both acid rain and respiratory problems, has been in effect 24 hours a day across the Delta, with some flares now having burnt continuously for 30 years. Since the early 1970s there have been complaints about Shell's slow and ineffectual response to issues of environmental safety and concern. Oil spills linked to poor maintenance have also destroyed fish-stocks in other hydrocarbon rich areas such as the enclave of Cabinda. Transnational corporation-led logging, mining, and farming have frequently destroyed land that has supported local communities for centuries, and displaced the local population by force and intimidation [Gibb, *Taming Transnationals: TNC exploitation of local communities around the world*, pr-log.org].

The Prize

How does it sound then if someone were to sum up the equation practically? Try this: "Corporatistan rules. Exxon Mobil is bigger than Turkey, Wal-Mart is bigger than Austria, GM is bigger than Indonesia, Daimler-Chrysler is bigger than Norway, BP is bigger than Thailand, Toyota is bigger than Venezuela, Citigroup is bigger than Israel and Total-Final-Elf is bigger than Iran. Ninety percent of the Corporatistan Top 500 is in the Triad. The Top 1000 account for no less than 80% of the world's industrial output" [Escobar, *Globalistan*, 27].

What is US industrial policy? It is to sell weapons, hence the unending wars everywhere. (It is a broader topic that all of this is for the gobalization merchants to retain control of the world's resources.) The playground, says Pepe, is every dictatorship's dream: "as BAE Systems sell their 72 Euro-fighters to Taliban-friendly Saudi Arabia—perhaps to bomb the next Shiite insurrection in Hasa—Lockheed Martin sells 36 F-16s to Taliban-friendly Pakistan—perhaps to be engulfed in the next scramble for Kashmir. . .the top 25 weapons clients of [the] US. . .[are] undemocratic regimes" [Escobar, *Globalistan*, Page 32].

The Strange Case of Lockheed Martin

William D Hartung, the director of the Arms and Security Initiative at the New America Foundation and the author of Prophets of War: Lockheed Martin and the making of the Military-Industrial Complex (Nation Books, January 2011), puts forward a scary narrative that might help us sum up a part of the picture of globalisation, that of the new power dynamics and the scope of big corporations. He argues that Lockheed Martin might as well actually run the US government. It received US$36 billion in government contracts in 2008 alone, more than any company in history, and that it now does work for more than two dozen government agencies, from the Department of Defense and the Department of Energy to the Department of Agriculture and the Environmental Protection Agency [tomdispatch.com].

Lockheed Martin is involved in surveillance and information processing for the CIA, FBI, IRS, NSA, Pentagon, Census Bureau, and Postal Service. It trains the agents of the Transportation Security Administration who provide security at the airports. It manufactures cluster bombs, designs nuclear weapons, and makes the F-35 Lightning (an overpriced, behind-schedule, under-performing combat aircraft that is slated to be bought by customers in more than a dozen countries). Recently it has virtually been running its own foreign policy, doing everything from hiring interrogators for US overseas prisons (including at Guantanamo Bay in Cuba and Abu Ghraib in Iraq) to managing a private intelligence network in Pakistan and helping write the Afghan constitution. The company receives one of every 14 dollars doled out by the Pentagon. In fact, it has a share of approximately $260 per taxpaying household in the United States. No weapons contractor has more money to wield to defend its turf, says Hartung.

It spends too. Lockheed Martin has spent $12 million on congressional lobbying and campaign contributions in 2009 alone. It ranks number one on the "contractor misconduct" database maintained by the Project on Government Oversight, a Washington DC-based watchdog group. From just a military contractor in the early 1990s, it has grown up into a juggernaut by racking up deals with the IRS, the Census Bureau, and the US Postal Service and other agencies, as a result of which it is now involved in nearly every interaction an American has with the government. From paying taxes to the national census, Lockheed Martin oversees a lot of things. For $500 million it is developing the Decennial Response Information Service (DRIS), which will collect and analyze information gathered from any source, from phone calls or the Internet to personal visits. It is in charge of the FBI's Integrated Automatic Fingerprint Identification System (IAFIS), a database of 55 million sets of fingerprints. The company also produces biometric identification devices that will identify people by scanning their iris, recognizing faces, or coming up with novel ways of collecting fingerprints or DNA. Since at least 2004, Lockheed Martin has been involved in the Pentagon's Counter-Intelligence Field Activity (CIFA), which collected personal data on American citizens for storage in a database known as "Threat and Local Observation Notice." While Congress shut down the domestic spying aspect of the program in 2007, CIFA itself continues to operate.

Lockheed Martin is also intimately bound up in the workings of the National Security Agency. In addition to producing spy satellites for NSA, the company is in charge of "Project Groundbreaker," a $5 billion, 10-year effort to upgrade the agency's internal telephone and computer networks. It has had a hand in recruiting election monitors for Bosnia and Ukraine, and in reforming Liberia's justice system. Lockheed Martin is the number-one contractor not only for the Pentagon, but also for the Department of Energy. It ranks number two for the Department of State, number three for the National Aeronautics and Space Administration, and number four for the Departments of Justice and Housing and Urban Development.

From manufacturing weapons to virtually ruling the lives of nearly every American, and also having a clout in other nations, Lockheed Martin is the poster boy of liquid modernity, where no boundaries are sacrosanct and no privacy is really private. When Eisenhower warned 50 years ago about the dangers of "unwarranted influence, whether sought or unsought, by the military-industrial complex," he probably meant this. A for-profit weapons outfit has fully integrated itself into a complex network of economic, social, and political structures, one in which no governmental activity is now beyond its reach, and possibly one which no single or multiple governmental agency can control. Liquid modernity, liquid power dynamics and the scope of modern corporations. If this is not scary, I do not know what is.

The Big Picture of Corporate Monopoly
Let us sample some more of Escobar's observations and intelligence-gatherings from his masterpiece book *Globalistan*:

1. The four world leaders in forest and paper products are all based in the U.S.

2. The five largest trading companies are all Japanese. The Japanese three biggest are Mitsui, Mitsubishi and Itochu, who deal with up to 30,000 products per company.

3. Fifty-six percent of the Fortune 500 is composed of commercial and savings banks. American, German and Japanese bank payments turn over the equivalent of their country's GDP every few days.

4. More than US$ 1.5 trillion move around the world every day in foreign exchange transactions;

5. 75% of the world's advertising is purchased in the Triad (as far as Asia is concerned this means Japan only).

6. Only seven companies dominate the global film market, and only five companies dominate the music industry.

7. Major U.S. TV and film studios collect up to 60% of their revenues overseas, the music business 70%.

8. Corporatistan—or the consumption of products made by Corporatistan—accounts for 50% of the gases responsible for global warming, and is the source of much of the world's toxic waste.

9. Two-thirds of hazardous waste produced in the U.S. comes from chemical corporations.

10. Corporatistan controls 50% of the world's oil, gas, coal mining, and
    refining.

Sameer Amin, in his article *The Battlefields Chosen by Contemporary Imperialism* writes that capitalism has reached a stage of gener-
alised oligopolies. While this is not a new phenomenon, "what is new
is the limited number of registered oligopolies or 'groups' which stands
at about 500, if only the colossal ones are counted. . .These chosen few
now determine the whole of economic life on the planet" [Amin, *The
Battlefields Chosen by Contemporary Imperialism*].

These days, the concept of modernity seems to determine nearly every aspect of this planet. But does this result in any better life for the
multitudes, since they "fell off the cosmic agenda centuries ago? 'By all
means,' says Capital, offering another warmed-up version of the 'trickle
down' theory, the principle that the poor, who must subsist on table
scraps dropped by the rich, can best be served by giving the rich bigger meals" [Blum, *Killing Hope, Part 1*, 19].

A "Trickle Down" Example: Dubai
A one-of-a-kind giant warehouse/tourist-and-shopping desti-
nation/transit point of global gold (legal or illegal) and al
Qaeda/Taliban/jihadi-network money at one edge of the Arabian
Peninsula, Dubai could well be termed a corporate neo-liberal dream.
Low taxes, right-less residency, artificial islands, yellow Ferraris, cheap
multicultural girls, along with steady labour from South Asia, Dubai is
a slap in the face of those who preach that Islam is not compatible with
Western ideologies. Pepe Escobar famously argues that the model spells
out an apolitical, consumer-mad, citizenship-free society, ideal for the
nomad elites of global modernity.

Of the 2.4 million people living there, only 15% are UAE citizens.
For the rest, it is immigration without citizenship—a smarter move over
the old fashioned U.S. headache of having to grant legitimacy to the Mex-
ican or Latin American immigrants. Liquid modernity does not like responsibility. As a result, the immigrants have to renounce their political
rights completely. While it does not present the elites even a whiff of
stale air, the catch-word for those at the bottom of the pyramid is an
old-fashioned expression: slave.

The slaves have no rights. Whether a construction worker or a cab driver or a counter salesman they are invisible—even though they comprise 80% of UAE's population. An average worker toils for around twelve hours a day in up to fifty degrees Celsius, and earns no more than $150 a month. He shares a small camp in some industrial suburb with 10-15 others. Living conditions are inhuman, and trade unions are banned. As long as he works in the UAE his passport is confiscated. He gets to go home once in two years. If he speaks up for any reason, he's instantly deported. If she's a woman and works as a maid or in a hotel, she can be sexually harassed—and there will be no consequences [Escobar, *Globalistan*, 71].

That is "trickle down" theory in practice. Dubai's medieval feudalistic approach is sold to the world as the most "progressive" state in the Middle East. Gold souks, expensive whiskeys, sports cars, and fast blond women take over the absence of rights to most people at the base of the billion dollar pyramid of luxury malls, condos, an artificial island, or some other tourist mini-paradise. Politics remains strictly off-limits. Consumerism rules. And post-modern Dubai continues to entice the rest of the world.

Conclusion

For a bottle of carbonated drink—celebrated as a symbol of the lifestyle of the West–this is a high price to pay. As the transnational companies jump business and operations from country to country with absolutely no regards for, or obligations to, the law of the land, we are left with a large number of poor nation states at the periphery. As the old solid productive capital or agricultural economy is phased out to make way for financial economy, and the political leaders stoop to new lows to clean the leather-boots of the hot-shots of liquid hyper-capitalism, the poor nations witness a series of implosions, rural unemployed people flooding to urban centres for survival being just one of them. But there are no jobs. So there is an increase in the crime rate, a steep rise in reactionary attitudes (invoking religion or ethnicity) in every facet of life, an increase in a victim complex for some, and an insane desire to mobilise and/or protest at everything. This only results in more domestic unrest, and that makes way for the implementation of new control measures, which in turn makes political parties and the corporate elite richer.

The globalisation-influenced interdependence cycle does not derive its basis from humanity. First there is greed; the rest is expendable. Always.

6 Battlefields of Oil—*The Greedster Effect on Energy Control*

After World War II, with domestic reserves already beginning to shrink, a succession of presidents fashioned a global strategy based on ensuring American access to overseas petroleum.

    —Michael T. Klare

It's no coincidence that the map of terror in the Middle East and Central Asia is practically interchangeable with the map of oil.

    —Pepe Escobar

In August of 1990 Saddam Hussein of Iraq invaded the neighbouring country of Kuwait. His goal was to add the enormous riches of the Kuwaiti oil fields to his already enviable position as one of the largest oil-producing nations of the world. If successful, he would have become the foremost global oil-dictator, dominating the Arab world and controlling the Persian Gulf. The world would have been at his mercy. The end justified the means.

We all know what happened after that. But what we find interesting is, over the previous several years, it was a rather common phrase among diplomatic and policy circles that oil was no longer important, so much so that in that very year (1990) the senior officers of America's Central Command were lectured on oil's waning strategic significance. This was not entirely accurate, because the invasion of Kuwait proved to be quite an eye-opener. "At the end of the twentieth century, oil was still central to security, prosperity, and the very nature of civilization." [Yergin, *The Prize*, 13].

Oil, the world's biggest and most omnipresent business, was hatched in the later half of the nineteenth century and soon after its birth managed to claim the crown of being the top dog and has remained so ever since. Oil is responsible for many of civilization's milestones. Even though the rise and development of capitalism in modern business happened before oil entered the stage, it was oil that facilitated the very first and largest among the multinational corporations of yesteryear—thus lending real-time legitimacy to capitalism in a few crucial ways. Oil as a commodity has formed an inseparable network of domestic and international policies and conflicts. "The battlefields of World War I established the importance of petroleum as an element of national power when the internal combustion machine overtook the horse and the coal-powered locomotive." Even afterwards, during World War II, Japan attacked Pearl Harbour to protect their oil resources in the East Indies, Hitler entered the USSR because he wanted the oil field of Caucasus—and the Allied forces ensured that by the end of the war German and Japanese fuel tanks were empty [Yergin, *The Prize*, 13]. After 1945 the US sponsored the election in Italy and ensured the defeat of the communists to ensure oil passage for its ships—and head-butted into the Middle East soon afterwards, triggering off a series of incidents, the fallout of which are ongoing even as this book gets written. And the same oil has transformed our individual lives, underpinning nearly everything that we mobile beings of the 21st century do. So you can guess at the import if some individual entity or corporation or nation-state exercises complete control over such a resource?

I do not need to tell you. The highly intriguing battle had uncertain beginnings with issues relating to availability, drilling, transportation, etc. John Rockefeller's Standard Oil was the first company to shoot into prominence during the 1860s. It would very soon go international by supplying its first cargo of kerosene oil to London. Working on Europe's sudden hunger for fuel oil, and gradually propelling his product into the fourth largest export of the entire American economy and first among manufactured goods—Rockefeller was the first person to establish oil as an international business.

Oil from the very beginning had the aura of phenomenal dimensions all around it. This was the business that one could not out-stare. Russians were the very next to jump into it. The Swedish family Nobel, emigrants to Russia during early 1800s, were the first to get into oil. Alfred went on to invent dynamite and facilitate the Nobel Prize legacy, Ludwig created a company called Nobel Wheels dealing in armaments supplying the

Russian Army, while the eldest son Robert went into oil. It was in the town of Baku where he bought his first refinery and officially put Russia in the business of oil. The year was 1873.

Competition and the Beginning of Conflict

Long-distance transit was a problem with oil. Wooden barrels, lengthy routes often being a mix of multiple sea and rail journies, enormous handling costs, unavailability of wood at times—all these led to a groundbreaking innovation that was to have a far-reaching impact. The Nobel brothers conceived the idea of shipping oil in bulk and by the mid 1880s oil transport underwent a major revolution as tankers started traversing the Atlantic.

Another issue was the fierce Russian winters that closed down ports, and also the affordability of illumination for the vast peasant population of the Russian empire. This eventually led the Nobel brothers to look for markets outside of Russia, while two other producers Bunge and Palashkovsky won government approval to build a railroad from Baku to Batum, a port on the Black Sea. But Bunge and Palashkovsky ran out of money due to a drop in oil prices and a French family stepped in to bail them out. They even arranged for transporting Russian oil to Europe. They were the Rothschilds. The Rothschild family was financially instrumental behind the railroad from Baku to be completed 1883, turning Batum into one of the world's most important oil ports. They, with the Nobel brothers closely behind them, quickly started building their storage and marketing facilities in Batum. The Baku-Batum railroad opened a door to the European West for Russian oil.

This series of initial activities was to initiate a fierce struggle for the oil markets of the world, which would not only be for monopoly in routes, distributions, markets, price, supply, and demand, but also trickle down to the tin containers that were then used to store kerosene oil. The war that would dominate human civilization for decades to come had begun.

The Present

Man's continued dependence and different nations' continued greed for the control of energy presents us with an interesting equation today. In the 21st century, with the threat of diminishing reserves of petroleum becoming more and more real, a chunk of the focus has shifted onto natural gas, as a result of which central Asian nations like Kazakhstan and Turkmenistan, erstwhile Soviet territories, have suddenly gained prominence with global leaders trying their best to buy their friendship. Most of the energy corporations are among the utmost vital entities of today's world, with the likes of the Russian giant Gazprom commanding a strong voice in the foreign policy of the country. There are an array of existing or proposed pipelines crisscrossing the entire length and breadth of central and south-western Asia. As a result of it, renewed power struggles, sometimes in the name of fighting terror and sometimes in the name of promoting democracy, have jumped into the forefront. And all along, issues relating to poverty or illiteracy or environmental degradation are being neglected completely. To cut into the issue, we need to look at four things: the geo-politics and strategic conduct of suddenly energy-rich states and their rulers, the proposed and the existing pipelines, the measures taken by the transnational corporations and nation-states to feed their energy greed, and the resultant state of affairs for the Asian population.

Understanding the Background of Present Conflicts

The key players are the oil and gas producers, the transit states through whose territories the pipelines (proposed and existing) run, and the existing or the aspiring global and regional powers that want to dominate the show. Close in tow are the oil and gas transnationals through a mechanism called Production Share Agreements, which means that technically the government may own its oil and gas but the oil corporations collect the wealth [platformlondon.org]. Interestingly, this industry has migrated from an entirely private birth and adolescence to now being jointly controlled by the governments and oil companies, emphasizing the fact that there is no better way to maximise private wealth and power other than by large scale state intervention.

The chief issue lies in control, because energy exercises absolute dominance across every aspect of our post-modern civilization, and controlling that would mean controlling the world. Ironically, all the oil/gas producing nations do not always have the amount of leverage that one tends to think. Yes they are important—primary in consideration, they are well paid and at times have high per-capita incomes, but landlocked countries like Kazakhstan or Turkmenistan have to depend heavily on the oil and gas pipelines that run through other countries in order to reach the global market. They do have control over the production process of their resources, but they do not always have complete control over the distribution mechanism, and practically whoever controls the pipelines controls the energy they contain. And that is where a scuffle is silently taking place—between Russia, China, Iran, and the United States.

The nations with key oil reserves in terms of ease of access are Saudi Arabia, Venezuela, Iran, Iraq, Kuwait, the UAE, Russia, Libya. and Nigeria [infoplease.com]. Though Canada has probably the second-largest oil reserves, the problem lies in the difficulty of extraction. (That brings us to another point that needs to be addressed here: it is not that the global oil stock is coming to an end, but the days of economically-feasible extraction of petroleum are). Therefore, the focus of global attention remains within the peripheries of central and south-west Asia. As fate would have it, the regions that produce most of the oil of the world are themselves or are neighbours to the regions that produce most of the natural gas too. In terms of gas, the most economically accessible gas sources are in and around central Asia. Kazakhstan and Turkmenistan have been mentioned before. Throw in Saudi Arabia, Iran, and Russia (again) along with Qatar, and you have the principles. It is assumed that the Caspian Sea holds less than 10% of Middle East reserves, but that is still vital because according to energy forecasts, "by 2050 the Persian Gulf/Caspian Sea will account for more than 80% of world oil and natural gas production." The storeroom is huge. Put together, the Persian Gulf and the Caspian hold about 800 billion barrels of oil and an energy-equivalent amount in natural gas. Oil reserves in the Americas and in Europe have less than 160 billion barrels, and that anyway would not last beyond 2030 [engforum.pravda.ru].

Central Asian oil and gas has historically flowed through Russian pipelines. Naturally Russia would want to retain that leverage. But that is where the others step in. China proposes to build a pipeline of about 3000 km from the Caspian oil fields across Kazakhstan and into China [Fishelson, *The Geopolitics of Oil Pipelines in Central Asia*]. It has to feed its growing economy in order to rise in power. Iran wants to pump the oil and gas south into its existing network. That would make Iran a leader in the Middle East, to the acute discomfort of Saudi Arabia—its oilfields have either peaked, or are close to peaking; plus northern Saudi Arabia's population is predominantly Shia, they draw moral endorsements from Iran. Starting with Lebanon, spreading slowly into Iraq, and currently Bahrain, the Shias have time and again demonstrated their resilience—naturally the Kingdom of Saudi Arabia (KSA) has every reason to feel jittery. The other power in concern is the US. The reason is a no-brainer.

Now for the logistics. Much of gas-rich central Asia until a few years ago was part of the Soviet empire. Development was nominal, and what little was done was done with a heavily centralised vision. For example, in Kazakhstan all roads and railroads were built northward into Russia and it was almost impossible to travel between the provinces of East and West Kazakhstan without a stop in Moscow. Even after independence, these states with their historical dependence on Russia carry on under the shadow of that mighty nation.

Apart from historic pride and prejudice, there are two more problems: geography and international relations. While geography plays a key role in central Asia, international relations or conflicts dominate the Middle East. This makes the pipelines and channels of distribution a challenge of sorts. For example, there is no easy route for central Asian oil and gas to reach shipping lanes and major markets such as Europe. One has to skirt the Caspian Sea and increase the length and number of transit nations (each of them charging a hefty fee for passage) or one has to build an underwater pipeline and multiply the cost many times. That is a geographical problem, which becomes a geopolitical issue if the same pipeline tries to run southeast towards the Indian Ocean, because in the middle of it then stands war-torn Afghanistan and the "Rogue State" of Pakistan [www.smh.com.au]. Each of the potential transit nations can charge quite a lot of money and also retains leverage in the potential threat of turning off the flow for political or economic reasons. Add to that the complication of numerous treaties, agreements, financial pacts, consortiums of governments and numerous oil companies more often than not at loggerheads with each other—and you have something of a mess. So far, there is only one surety, that of the alignment of Saudi

Arabia and Kuwait with the United States. That has been so for some time. Both the governments and the oil corporations have consolidated over the years. However, the other oil and gas-rich nations are either in a state of turmoil or under the rule of eccentric and often unpredictable autocrats—and that makes it a complete mess.

The Caspian Sea

One exemplary conflict among many is the controversy over whether the Caspian should be classified as a lake or a sea under the United Nation's Convention on the Law of the Sea (1982). As of today, Russia and Iran consider it a lake, while Azerbaijan, Turkmenistan, and Kazakhstan prefer a sea classification. Under the 1921 Friendship Treaty between Persia (now Iran) and the USSR, the Caspian was divided between those two states. While Russia and Iran consider this treaty valid, Azerbaijan, Kazakhstan, and Turkmenistan do not agree to the arrangement—and the deadlock continues. Although the issue of ownership remains undecided, oil and gas exploration and drilling continue with abandon [Fishelson, *The Geopolitics of Oil Pipelines in Central Asia*].

Washington's Pipeline Gambits

The first brawl was when NATO forces flew war-planes to the Balkans and bombed Yugoslavia. And kept bombing. Thousands of people died as a result. The US President expressed serious concerns, and sent some more bombs. The logic was that NATO was fighting to liberate the Albanians in Kosovo. Looking past the grotesque notion of "bombing you to liberate you," it was an opportunity for the US-based Albanian Macedonian Bulgarian Oil Corporation (AMBO) to build a $1.1 billion pipeline to bring Caspian Basin oil to the West, thus bypassing Iran and Russia [wikipedia.org]. The AMBO pipeline, once operational, was supposed to transport Caspian Basin oil via Georgia, Turkey, Bulgaria, Macedonia, and Albania. But Bulgaria pulled out in the middle due to energy concerns.

The scuffle was about to get worse.

In May, 2005, high-quality Caspian light crude oil started flowing through the Caucasus towards the Mediterranean Sea port in Turkey. The Baku-Tbilisi-Ceyhan (BTC) pipeline—hailed by many as marking the end of US dependence on the Persian Gulf—originated in Baku, thence to Azerbaijan, through Tbilisi in Georgia, and finally to Ceyhan, Turkey. This was greed glorified: "a supreme law unto itself, untouchable by national sovereignty, serious environmental concerns, labour legislation and protests against the World Bank"; and oblivious to geography of mountains or rivers. BTC took 10 years and US$ 4 billion, and it enjoys "rights in some ways superior to those of a sovereign state." It spans six war zones (Nagorno-Karabakh, Chechnya, Dagestan, Ossetia, Abkhazia and Turkish Kurdistan), two extremely volatile countries (Georgia and Azerbaijan), a secessionist province (Ajaria)—and it is another slap in the face to the ignorant masses who think that conflicts in Asia are over ideologies [Escobar, *Globalistan*, 42–43].

The major shareholders of BTC are British Petroleum, SOCAR of the Azerbaijan government, Unocal of the US, Statoil of Norway, Turkish Petroleum, ENI of Italy, TotalFinaElf of France, Itochu of Japan, ConocoPhillips of the US, Inpex of Japan, and a joint venture called Delta Hess—the list is overcrowded with the Triad nations' oil corporations. BP is said to have signed an agreement that is "no less than an international treaty to back its investment." By nature an Inter-Governmental Agreement (IGA) between Azerbaijan, Georgia and Turkey, "these agreements have largely exempted BP and its partners from any laws in the three countries—present or future—which conflict with the company's project plans. The agreements allow BP to demand compensation from the governments should any law (including environmental, social or human rights law) make the pipeline less profitable." Then, in the case of Turkey, BTC effectively trisects the state into three: "the area where Turkish law applies; the Kurdish areas under official or *de facto* military rule; and a strip running the entire length of the country from North to South where BP is the effective government" [Escobar, *Globalistan*, 44].

This hyper-hyped project has been possible in part because of Hayder Aliyev, the ruthless, US-supported dictator of Azerbaijan. After his death in 2003 his son Ilham assumed power, continuing a dynastic autocracy. He is also the head of SOCAR, the state oil company, a major player in BTC. This regime stands at a low of 140 out of 146 nations in the global perceived corruption index—a study done by Transparency International. But to U.S. policy makers, the self-proclaimed torchbearers of global liberty and democracy, Ilham Aliyev is "their son of a bitch."

The BTC spells power politics in bold. Despite its size and scope, this pipeline is not economical. Oil experts unanimously agree that a Caspian exit route through Russia or Iran is more cost-effective. That is exactly where the point lies: BTC is seen as the global ambition of the triad to bypass Russia and Iran to supply to the West. Add to that the middle eastern state of Israel just across the Mediterranean coast of Turkey and the possibility of a small underwater extension of the BTC—or a ferrying line of oil tankers—and BTC gets an entry into the Asian market as well.

What about the local population? Well, Georgia lives on American alms; and Azeri families, first rejected by Soviets and then by liquid modernity, remain incredibly poor with little or no water and electricity. They co-exist beside the super-rich expatriates driving their SUVs. "The only other flourishing industry in the Caucasus, apart from oil, is kidnapping," observes Pepe Escobar.

The second major US pipeline project is the Trans-Caspian Pipeline (TCP). This proposed project would be a gas, oil, or combined pipeline. It would go from Kazakhstan and/or Turkmenistan under the Caspian Sea to Baku, Azerbaijan. From there, any oil could link with the existing BTC pipeline to ultimately access the Mediterranean, while the gas could be transported via the South Caucasus gas pipeline into eastern Turkey. The oil or gas would thereby be brought into the open market. The TCP has the potential to bypass political complications, as it would be burrowed under the Caspian. That in turn would make it a lot more expensive. For this reason it is said that the TCP would make sense only if it is a combined oil-gas affair. The initial problem was in finding investors, not that there was a dearth of them, but Turkmenistan's historical unpredictability in it's relations with the US and the West complicated that [Fishelson, *The geopolitics of oil pipelines in Central Asia*].

Not anymore. After the death of president Saparmurat Niyazov, the new Turkmen president, Gurbanguli Berdymukhamedov, has not explicitly addressed the TCP, but has promised reforms. To the multitude of Turkmen population, roughly 70% of them unemployed, 44% living under US$ 2 a day in what is considered to be one of the most closed former Soviet Bloc societies with no public health, political opposition, or media independence, these reforms make no sense, and Turkmenistan, the third-largest producer and the second-largest exporter of natural gas in the world, with all its wealth, still does not have decent roads or an effective police department [libraryindex.com].

Russian Roulette

In geo-strategic parlance, central Asia is Russia-dependent. From its history to its economy, from roads to the common border with central Asian states, Russia is a major player who cannot be overruled. A small pipeline network built by the Soviets has long carried Central Asian oil and gas towards Moscow. However, this network was not sufficient to carry the massive amount of reserves that were available. After the fall of the Soviet Union, the new states built three more pipelines: "the Caspian Pipeline Consortium from the Tengiz oil fields to the Russian port of Novorossiysk on the Black Sea; the Korpezhe-Kurt Kui gas pipeline from the Turkmen fields to Iran; and the Kazakhstan-China pipeline from Atasu to Alataw in China" [Fishelson, *The Geopolitics of Oil Pipelines in Central Asia*].

Gazprom, headquartered in Moscow, accounts for nearly 20% (some sources say 25%) of world gas production, with a 25% share in European markets. It is the world's largest natural gas company. Along with German companies E.O.N. and BASF, it is building the 1200-kilometer Nord Stream Pipeline to carry natural gas from Vyborg, near St. Petersburg, under the Baltic Sea to Greifswald in eastern Germany, "which will increase the amount of fuel available in Germany by 28%. The pipeline will inevitably be extended to the Netherlands and Britain as well" [Escobar, *Globalistan*, 49]. The first leg is to be operational from late 2011. And to continue the story, Gazprom also intends building Blue Stream 2, a new pipeline under the Black Sea, to deliver gas to Turkey, Greece and Italy, and involve transit countries like Bulgaria, Romania, Hungary and Austria. Once this is operational, Europe can forget BTC—it will be Russian gas all over. Europe, the largest trading block in the world, is the fair-lady again, being courted by both the US and Russia. The way things stand, Russia is capitalizing on its advantage.

Looking eastwards, Russia has taken China, Japan, and Korea into orbit through the Russian pipeline-maker Transneft, which built the East Siberian Pacific Ocean (ESPO) Pipeline. "The ESPO pipeline will carry up to 1.6 million barrels of crude oil each year from Siberia to Russia's eastern border, then into China and the Asia-Pacific region. The first part of the pipeline linked Taishet in eastern Siberia to Skovorodino in the far east of Russia. This section runs for 1,713 miles and has an annual capacity of 220 million barrels. Stage two of ESPO will carry 367.5 million barrels annually from Skovorodino to the Pacific, a distance of 1,304 miles. The first part of the ESPO pipeline was opened in October 2008 and ran for 680 miles in the far eastern republic of Yakutia. The pipeline became fully operational in December 2009" [ezinearticles.com]. The bonus is that the control of oil flow remains with Russia.

The Iranian Dilemma

Iran is in a fix. It has 13% of the world's total fossil fuel reserves, which makes it the second-largest oil-and-gas rich country in the world and second-largest OPEC producer, behind Saudi Arabia. According to the Petroleum Ministry's own estimates, Iranian oil will last from seventy to a maximum of eighty-six years while gas may last longer than two hundred years. But Iran has to import refined products. And if this continues, Iran will be forced to suspend its oil exports before 2020. If you are wondering why, it is chiefly because of American sanctions. There are a couple of related reasons too. Iran, due to years of involuntary isolation, does not have relations with many other nations, which has led to a lack of investors. Most of the installations that were destroyed by Iraqi forces during the Iran-Iraq war of the 1980s are in much the same condition. Finally, there are countries like India who, in return for partly-imaginary improved relations with the US, has abandoned previously proposed joint projects with Iran, including a pipeline called IPI [Escobar, *Globalistan*, 50].

But the disengagement of countries like India is just part of the problem, and though it is crucial, Iran currently has gas pipelines to Armenia, Azerbaijan, and a proposed project called Persian Pipeline or IGAT9, to carry gas to Turkey and to the European states of Greece and Switzerland. The key thing now for Iran is to attract investors, which has been difficult since Bill Clinton signed the Iran and Libya Sanctions Act of

1996. About the time the BTC pipeline was being hyped, Iran proposed an oil pipeline between Iran, Iraq, and Syria. "Iran thus can swap Caspian Sea crude to be refined in the country and then deliver the final product to the Mediterranean. The killer argument: as far as both Asian and European customers are concerned, the cost of using this pipeline route is way lower than using BTC—a fact that even American oil industry insiders recognised long ago" [Escobar, *Globalistan*, 51].

And if that is not enough to upset the US there is more: Iran pulled Iraq to the table to negotiate the construction of a pipeline between Abadan, in southern Iran, and Basra, in southern Iraq. They have signed an agreement following which Iraq will send crude from Basra to be refined in Abadan, and in exchange will get oil derivatives. Iraq's refineries are inadequate, thanks to the American bombs. The Iraqi government is Shia dominated—a consequence of the American obsession with killing the Ba'athist Sunni population during the Gulf crisis. Saudi Arabia now is seeing an axis of Shia all around the Middle East, and probably that is why the Sunni guerrillas keep sabotaging the Iraqi pipelines to delay the Iran-Iraq oil and gas integration, even despite the American presence in the region [Escobar, *Globalistan*, 51].

A great prize that Iran could have won was a deal with China. China does not bother much about US sanctions. And the US grudgingly accepts the fact. The Kazakhstan-China Pipeline, owned by CNPC China and KazMunayGas Kazakhstan, China's first direct oil import pipeline from the Caspian was completed in 2009 and runs 2228 km from Atyrau to Alashankou. "China imports nearly 50% of its oil, mostly from the Middle East. The Iraq war was a graphic demonstration to the leadership in Beijing that Washington will pull no punches to control and militarise whatever of the world's major oil and gas sources it may lay its hands on. So, inevitably for China, central Asia and the Caspian became absolutely crucial." Tehran followed suit and signed a $100 billion gas deal with Beijing. "Iran will export 10 million tons of liquefied natural gas (LNG) a year from its Yadavaran field for a 25-year period while China's state oil company Sinopec will invest in exploration, drilling, petrochemical and gas industries, pipelines and services in Iran." Once oil investment comes into the picture, the deal gets to become $200 billion [Escobar, *Globalistan*, 61–62].

While India remains unsure and insignificant as always in matters of international relations, China has also shown keen interest about the proposed IPI, or Iran-Pakistan-India pipeline, also once upon a time dubbed by rhetoric-loving governments as the "Peace Pipeline." The pipeline was supposed to exploit South Pars, a giant gas field containing "9% of the world's proven reserves." With the controversy going on for "10 years", now Pakistan has expressed its desire to cut the last 'I' out of IPI and replace it with a 'C' [Escobar, *Globalistan*, 63]. China is very happy with the arrangement. Iran, with everything to gain, also probably agrees silently. India waits for HMV (His Master's Voice). Diligently.

Iran is moving sure-footedly to get out of its historic disadvantage. As this book gets written, Tehran is on track to become a member of the Shanghai Cooperative Organization (SCO). It is not an 'if' anymore; it is a 'when.' When that happens Iran will become a member of the Asian Energy Security Grid by default—and these two are considered a counter-balance to US ambition in Asia. It has also exported about nine billion cubic meters of natural gas to Europe during the past 11 months, setting a new record [lngworldnews.com]. We might also see non-Triad foreign direct investment flowing into the country in the near future. This all without US support—in fact with the US trying to sabotage every initiative wholeheartedly. A final relevance of Iran is that it is in a favourable geographical position. The Persian Gulf allows the easiest outlet for the central Asian pipelines to the rest of the world, and the warmer climate allows year-long unimpeded access. Iran is also economically weaker than Russia; naturally the costs of construction and maintenance are also lower. US policy makers must be having regular nightmares of President Ahmedinejad in a green suit peeping through their bedroom windows.

The Prize of Iraq

Iraq holds the world's second-largest known oil reserves. Unexplored oil fields account for roughly 60% of Iraq's known reserves. The al-Majnoon megafield alone holds an estimated 20 billion barrels. If Exxon Mobil, for instance, "got" al-Majnoon its global reserves would instantly double [Escobar, *Globalistan*, 66]. So "democracy" or "defeating the insurgency" was never the issue; Iraq was all about feeding the US's greed system. They are motivated by the fact that Saudi Arabian and Kuwaiti oil is already peaking or threatening to peak. Iran is a taboo. central Asian oil/gas is a kitchen with too many cooks in it. It will take a while to cool down. Iraq it was.

This was brought about systematically. First, Saddam was subtly prompted to invade Kuwait. April Glaspie, the US Ambassador to Iraq during 1980-88, reportedly told Saddam Hussein, "We have no opinion on your Arab-Arab conflicts, such as your dispute with Kuwait. Secretary Baker has directed me to emphasise the instruction, first given to Iraq in the 1960s, that the Kuwait issue is not associated with America" [walt.foreignpolicy.com]. This gave Saddam the "green light" to invade Kuwait.

Then "Iraq was starved and decimated by 12 years of U.N. sanctions," following which "it was Shocked and Awed into oblivion." Then one of the puppet governments, "on the road to 'democracy' " was forced to ask the US Treasury Department-dominated IMF for a "US$ 685 million loan to rebuild what the U.S. shocked and awed." The IMF in turn "forced Iraq to scrap oil subsidies and privatise the economy." Unemployment rocketed to 70%. The IMF did some more "structural adjustments." It dismantled the essential "social services in Iraq under which Saddam's oil money paid for some of the best hospitals and universities in the Middle East" [Escobar, *Globalistan*, 67].

The United Nations estimates that a third of the Iraqi population lives below the poverty line. A 2004 survey of Iraqi living conditions conducted by the U.N. and Iraq's Ministry of Planning and Development found that "by 2004, Iraqi living standards had deteriorated considerably compared with that of the 1970s and '80s, particularly in the areas of water, electricity, sanitation, jobs, income and assets... 85% of households lacked a stable source of electricity, with weekly and even daily outages... Nearly 70% of households struggled with getting rid of garbage... more than 40% had inadequate sanitation facilities... Poverty levels were three times higher in rural areas... American free-market priorities dismantled state-run enterprises that employed hundreds of thousands of Iraqis and ended subsidies" [latimes.com].

For oil giants like Exxon Mobil or Chevron, it has become really crucial now to have oil reserves as part of their assets. The oil industry is gradually transforming into producing or innovating "greener fossil fuels" by blending diesel with a cleaner new hybrid of diesel and natural gas or diesel with ethanol and bio-diesel. Diversification in their main vertical is something that the archaic oil industry is not used to, but nonetheless they have to find other ways to make money. "Astronomic profits for Big Oil only apply when Big Oil controls oil fields—and new oil fields are getting scarcer by the day. . . It's by owning oil fields that Exxon Mobil's 2005 profit can reach US$ 32 billion, the largest single profit in the history of Corporatistan" [Escobar, *Globalistan*, 68]. And Iraq offered a way out—not only in terms of big money, but also in terms of big power.

Well, this was the plan. Let us look at the result of the US/NATO invasion of Iraq a little more closely.

The United States invaded Iraq in 2003 with three goals: the destruction of the Iraqi army; the destruction of the Ba'athist regime; and the replacement of that regime with a stable, pro-American government in Baghdad to secure its oil supply. The first two goals were achieved in a jiffy. The third however continues to elude them, even after 8 long years [stratfor.com].

In their haste to annihilate the Ba'athist Sunnis, the Americans made the anti-Ba'athist, Iran-influenced Shi'ite community the main face of Iraq. The Sunnis, stuck between a rock and a hard place, launched an insurgency against both—taking active support from foreign mercenaries. The result of it was the Sunnis fighting the Shias and US forces; a near war situation between the US and the Iran-dominated Shias; the Sunnis fighting the Kurds (a legacy from the times of Saddam Hussein)—a complex civil war, in short, with the US participating in it. The Americans opted for a compromise. They argued that they wanted a stable government; not necessarily a pro-US one, but at least not, certainly, pro-Iran. Too late. They had destroyed a government, an army, and a people that they could not recreate.

With Iraq's unwillingness to grant a special status to the US forces that exempted them from Iraqi justice, and more importantly because of the mounting domestic pressure, the US finally moved out of Iraq. And that brought an interesting angle to the Middle East equation. The US withdrawal has made Iran the most powerful conventional power in the

Persian Gulf. The historical balance of power had been between Iraq and Iran. After Shock and Awe, that balance was destroyed. Iran, for its experience of a devastating war with a US-backed Iraq, would want to make certain that Iraq remained weak and divided. Iran would also justifiably want to seize upon the opportunity of trying to geopolitically align a Shia dominated Iraq with itself. At this point they have the ability to influence an Iraqi government in both ways; firebrand Iraqi Shia leaders like Muqtada al Sadr are a living testimony to that.

In July of 2010, after months of chaos, Iraqi Prime Minister Nuri al-Maliki struck a deal with a Shia livewire—the chubby faced thirty-something rebel Muqtada al-Sadr—under the watchful eye of the Iranians. Reportedly, the deal says that "the powerful Shi'ite leader will drop his veto over Maliki's continuation of the premiership, in exchange for... an amnesty setting hundreds of members of Muqtada's Mahdi Army free... greater (Sadrist) representation, and more power within the government, with crucial ministries like the ones they held in 2006–2008; Education, Commerce and Health... in addition Maliki will protect Muqtada from government persecution, allowing his men to maintain arms in the suburbs of Baghdad, while Muqtada will use his tremendous influence among young and poor people within the Shi'ite community to further legitimise and popularise the prime minister... If Maliki backs out on any of his promises, Muqtada will withdraw support and bring down Maliki's cabinet" [Sami Moubayed, *Mercurial Maliki on cusp of retaining power*, Asia Times, 20.07.2010].

With Iraq getting tangled progressively in Iran's geopolitical manoeuvres, the United States now, after its withdrawal, has three straight choices. The first one is to leave Iran in control and seriously jeopardise two things: the control of oil and gas and its relationship with Saudi Arabia and Israel. The second one is to go ahead and declare a war against Iran; clearly not a bad idea, because economic sanctions against the "evil state" are not helping. The third one is to destabilise Iraq yet again, this time tilting the balance against Prime Minister Maliki and the Shias—a process that some suspect has begun already [MK Bhadrakumar, *US Turkey and Iraqi Kurds Join Hands*, Asia Times 24.04.2012]. There is a fourth choice—negotiating with Iran. Or is it a choice at all? We do not know for sure. But whenever there are transnational corporations involved we have learnt that geo-economics always triumphs over geo-politics.

The Trans Afghan Pipeline (TAP/TAPI)

Turkmen president-for-life Turkmenbashi "Sun-King" Saparmurat Niya-zov (19 February 1940–21 December 2006) left quite an imprint. While he was alive and in power, he banned every form of opposition to his rule, whether secular or Islamic. He banned all political parties. He kept the media under complete control. Group meetings of any kind were forbidden. Prison torture was endemic and dissent could be punishable by death. "In this authoritarian presidentialism. . . coupled with the myth of a strong state. . . (his personality cult) would make any Hollywood—or Washington—spin doctor green with envy" [Escobar, *Globalistan*, 56].

The country however does not have good roads to speak of, and it has an extremely poor population comprised chiefly of illiterate and ignorant central Asian tribes with nomadic traces in them. What it has in plenty is incredibly rich concentrations of oil and natural gas—enough for the Big Brothers to jump in.

Turkmenistan is strategically located. It can supply gas to Russia (North), to Iran (South), to China (East) and to Turkey (West). However, with historic ties to Russia there was a slight inclination favouring them. In early September 2006, Gazprom finally accepted "the 40% price increase" demanded by the Sun-King for his gas. What Russia got in return for this deal was mind boggling. It was given control of Turkmenistan's entire gas surplus up to 2009, a preference to explore the new Yolotan gas fields, and the "Turkmenbashi saying he was out of any future Trans-Caspian pipeline project" [Escobar, *Globalistan*, 59].

Much of this changed after the death of Turkmenbashi. With new President Gurbanguly Berdymukhamedov the South Yolotan field for instance went to Chinese, UAE, and South Korean companies for development. Then came the global meltdown and the near bankruptcy of the EU. The prior arrangements with Gazprom crumbled. Russia refused to pay European prices for Turkmen gas. The demand was low in Europe and several large gas fields were coming online in Russia, which could effectively reduce its need for central Asian gas. "The Yamal Peninsula deposit alone is estimated to hold roughly 16 trillion cubic meters of gas. Yamal can easily feed both the North Stream (55 bcm at full capacity) and South Stream (63 bcm at full capacity) pipelines and still have a surplus" [MK Bhadrakumar, *Pipeline project a new silk road*, Asia Times 16.12.2010]. That made much of Turkmenistan production suddenly irrelevant—at least for the northern part of its map.

With the improved relations with the West, the once-champion paper-tiger project, the Trans Afghan Pipeline, a.k.a. the Turkmenistan-Afghanistan-Pakistan Pipeline, a.k.a. the Turkmenistan-Afghanistan-Pakistan-India (TAPI) Pipeline—that has been bobbing up and down for quite some time now—occupied the centre stage of the oil-war again. The announced 1,000-mile route is supposed to follow the ancient trading route from central to south Asia, extending from the Dauletabad gas field in Turkmenistan along the highway through Herat, Helmand, and Kandahar in Afghanistan, to Quetta and Multan in Pakistan, and on to Fazilka in India.

The TAPI has been the single most vital ambition of the United States in this battle for control. The implications are many. A gas pipeline from Turkmenistan to Pakistan via Afghanistan can open up the entire Western market and significantly reduce Europe's energy dependence on Russia. This is a route that goes neither through Russia, nor Iran, nor China. It is not nearly as expensive as the BTC. A line can be channelled into India to feed the growing nation's huge and hungry market. It can end India's and Pakistan's growing intimacy with Iran, the result of which could be the potentially "dangerous" proposed IPI Pipeline. The Pakistan deep-water port of Gwadar, where the pipeline is supposed to terminate, is an ideal candidate for year-round uploading—a Dubai-in-waiting. Overall, this pipeline increases the US influence in South Asia tremendously. These are the reasons why the US has been promoting the TAPI pipeline since the 1990s, when the Taliban was in power.

Two consortia, one led by UNOCAL (US) and the other by Bridas (Argentina), initially competed for the project. The US government supported the UNOCAL consortium for obvious reasons. An article from Counterpunch by Tom Turnipseed (2002) reads:

Beneath their burkas, UNOCAL is being exposed for giving the 5-star treatment to Taliban Mullahs in the Lone-Star State in 1997. The "evil-ones" were also invited to meet with U.S. government officials in Washington, D.C. The article further documents that. . . [At] the same time, U.S. government documents reveal that the Taliban were harbouring Osama bin Laden as their "guest" since June 1996. By then, bin Laden had: been expelled by Sudan in early 1996 in response to US insistence and the threat of UN sanctions; publicly declared war against the U.S. on or about August 23, 1996; pronounced the bombings in Riyadh and at Khobar in Saudi Arabia killing 19 US servicemen as "praiseworthy terrorism", promising that other attacks would follow in November 1996 and further admitted carrying out attacks on U.S. military personnel in Somalia in 1993 and Yemen in 1992, declaring that "we used to hunt them down in Mogadishu"; stated in an interview broadcast in February 1997 that "if someone can kill an American soldier, it is better than wasting time on other matters" [counterpunch.org].

At that time, the UNOCAL consultant was none other than the current President of Afghanistan, Hamid Karzai. It is probably an insignificant fact here that Bridas (then competing with UNOCAL) got brought over later. In August of 1997, a cash-flow crisis forced Bridas to sell off 60% of its stock to Amoco, which later got merged with British Petroleum. A key consultant to Amoco during those days was the CIA poster-boy, the Grand Chessboard proponent, contemporary US foreign policy makers' favourite, and the friend of Osama bin Laden—Zbignew Brzezinski.

While this pipeline clearly augments Turkmenistan's cause of finding a new market for its now surplus gas, it benefits Pakistan and India too. Pakistan is looking at a looming energy crisis. It actually looks at a multitude of crises, but we will address them over a different platform. The TAPI can bail it out. Then, it is also eyeing a hefty amount from India as transit fee. In addition to the usual economic benefits such as industrial expansion, job creation etc., the TAPI involves the US, and Pakistan's government is always very comfortable with anything American.

The Problems. . .

. . .are many. At the top resides Afghanistan. TAPI is supposed to cover the conflict-stricken areas of Herat, Helmand, and Kandahar in

Afghanistan, along with certain Pakhtun tracts in the frontier. The key therefore is in neutering the nation. It was initially sought through courting the Taliban. When talks failed because the Talibs demanded an exorbitant amount as transit fees, at a Group of Eight Summit in Genoa, "Western diplomats indicated that the Bush administration had decided to take the Taliban down before year's end" [Escobar, *Pipelinestan goes Af-Pak*, Asia Times 14.05.2009]. That was July of 2001. Small wonder, 9/11 happened in a few months and Big Brother got an iron-clad reason to attack the hapless Pakhtuns.

The game in Eurasia is constantly shifting. Just when things were looking up for the Gazprom guys, with all the Turkmen gas and the huge geography of Europe to cater to, things changed. Just like that, the sudden revival of TAPI threw Afghanistan again into the limelight. Historically this has been a crucial place for America—a buffer-zone between Russia and Iran. With the looming energy crisis, with China gobbling up everything in its way, with Russia posing a comeback, control of energy-rich central Asia and cash-rich south Asia is seen as essential to future US global power. A US presence here could put both Russia and China on the defensive. The strategy, for a long time has been building a continuous patchwork of American protectorates along the Persian Gulf, Black Sea and Caspian Sea region. Afghanistan is just one of them situated very conveniently as a key link between central and south Asia, spot in the middle of the four nuclear powers of India, Iran, Pakistan, and China, and apparently has unexplored rich deposits of "natural gas, petroleum, coal, copper, chrome, talc, barites, sulphur, lead, zinc, and iron ore, as well as precious and semiprecious stones" [Escobar,, *Pipelinestan goes Af-Pak* Asia Times 14.05.2009]. Add to that the world famous Afghan heroin trade that works only on US dollars, not Euros. So, if you thought the Taliban, al Qaeda, or whoever was why Afghanistan was under attack, think again.

After relentlessly pounding the Afghan land and population for years, and yet failing miserably to achieve any of its proposed goals of a) catching bin Laden (who was later found hiding in Pakistan) and b) removing the Taliban from power, the US now, under the new president Obama's leadership, has suddenly produced the 'good' Taliban from inside of a magician's hat—and his government wants to talk to them about possible power sharing in Kabul. The details can be found in any news-paper.

The next problem is Pakistan. In fact, the strange pattern in TAPI is, out of the four nations in this gas-relay race, the opener and the final-leg runner –Turkmenistan and India, though notoriously at the bottom of the global ranking list of Transparency International – still seem reasonably fit to sprint. The two runners in the middle, Afghanistan and Pakistan are quite dicey. Pakistan is a rogue state. At least there is some stan-dardization in Afghan behaviour—the fact that only Talibans/Pakhtuns might blow up the pipelines. In the state of Pakistan, anyone can. From the quite long list of fundamentalist outfits that form a permanent fixture in socio-political Pakistan, anyone can walk up and blow a big hole in the pipeline. There has never been a dearth of reasons. From expressing their resentment against the minorities or a grudge against the Americans or NATO, the pipeline can be treated as a multiple demonstration point by them. In fact, there have been a few cases of late, those that did not receive much newspaper coverage; the only exception probably was the Baluchistan Times.

Another issue is a place in Pakistan called Gwadar. It was built mainly by Chinese money and involvement (by the China Harbour En-gineering Company), and is currently in the possession of the Port of Singapore Authority (PSA). The US and China are said to have their eyes on this place. It is a deep-sea port in the secessionist Baluchistan province, which is much like the small village that Dubai was before it began setting up free Trade Zones for select business categories. The issue is that a sudden theoretical proliferation of oil and gas pipelines along the power corridors of the world has shaken the sleepy village up, and it is now in the middle of a tug-of-war. The US needs Gwadar for the TAPI. Until recently it was known that China needed Gwadar for a future pipeline, possibly from Iran (possibly a variant of the proposed IPI). There have been some very recent changes in the Chinese stance, after Pakistan tried to warm-up to them to prove a few points to the US, and they have denied having designs on Gwadar.

Practically, Gwadar has been a non-starter so far, surviving on or-chestrated carriage diversions from the port of Karachi, at a huge cost—to the chagrin of Karachi port authorities. The PSA are not keen to stick around any longer, and Pakistan is desperately looking for new suitors. The local Baluch population, secessionist in nature, do not like the Chinese because of what they perceive to be a high-handed Chinese attitude that involves overlooking the interest of the locals in their dealing with Islamabad—a government that supports terrorising and oppressing Baluchistan ever since Pakistan forcibly occupied their sovereign territory in 1948 [huffingtonpost.com, telegraph.co.uk]. No one listens to them as usual. Weighing everything carefully, Gwadar and indeed the entire Baluchistan province looks like another ticking time bomb. But because big money has never traditionally bothered with the "rascal multitude," the Pakistani government and the brotherhood of the ISI and the army keep suppressing, illegally abducting, or detaining and killing the Baluch people at one hand, and on the other keep pitching about Gwadar to anyone relevant [tribune.com.pk]. TAPI, IPI, or some Iranian-Chinese pipeline via Baluchistan; changes in the American or the Chinese attitude towards them—Pakistan, as a nearsighted nation seems hell bent on taking the easy way out. The transit money is huge—threats of secession, dwindling economy, bomb blasts killing ill-fated civilians, stone-cold illiterate security guard assassinating his governor, murdering of the minority affairs minister Shahbaz Bhatti, and the torture-murder of journalists be damned [bbc.co.uk, nytimes.com].

India is comparatively more stable than Pakistan or Afghanistan, but it suffers from a different malady. It is called "US-beckons-India-follows" syndrome (I discovered this disease with a hint from an M.K. Bhadrakumar article). The United Progressive Alliance government is obediently following the footsteps left behind by the United States in its walk towards TAPI, scrapping IPI in the whole process—despite the fact that TAPI is fraught with practical and political problems. Earlier IPI was known as the "Peace Pipeline"; not anymore. Now TAPI is the new Peace Pipeline, and IPI does not have a name. Jeopardizing relations with key Asian neighbours also probably does not have any name. The last one was Hindi-Chini-bhai-bhai [wikipedia.org]. At the beginning of March 2011, The Telegraph (Calcutta) came out with a small report about the Indian Prime Minister writing a personal letter to the Iranian President expressing solidarity with Iran—a few months after which New Delhi announced a cut in oil imports from Iran [KP Nayar, *Delhi builds Tehran line*, telegraphindia.com].

The US has made its stance very clear. It does not want to move out from Afghanistan, not at least before some pro-US government comes to power there. That looks unlikely. Hamid Karzai controls little outside of Kabul. "Good" Taliban might be a possible option. But like the transnational corporations, the Taliban too has gone international. From Afghanistan it has branched off to Pakistan with the new operative name Tehrik e Taliban Pakistan (TTP)—probably with a vision to corporatise terrorism with a little help from their real estate provider and sponsor. (They even have a Shura or consultative council called Quetta Shura). Pakistan thus enters the equation again as the local-guardian of this new breed.

The new united Pakistani Taliban has a central emir, his deputies and lieutenants—the whole fitment. In the beginning, "some of the key militant groups that joined the TTP conglomerate by pledging allegiance to Baitullah (Mehsood) and submitted themselves to his centralised command included the Tehrik-e-Nifaz-e-Shariat-e-Mohammadi (TNSM) led by Maulvi Fazlullah; the Hafiz Gul Bahadur group of the Taliban in North Waziristan; the Maulvi Nazir group of the Taliban in South Waziristan; the Tehrike Taliban of Omar Khalid, both factions of the Tehrike Tuleba led by Mullah Safi and Mullah Jalali respectively; the Islamic Movement of Uzbekistan (IMU) led by Tahir Yuldashev; the Tora Bora Taliban created by Maulvi Khalis; and the Lashkar-e-Mohammadia" [atimes.com].

The Taliban, referred to as "rag-tag militia" by Western policy makers and media, actually has divided the tribal areas along the Pakistan side of the Durand Line into administrative zones (it is a substantial stretch), each looked after by an appointed commander that reports to the supreme commander of the local Taliban and the consultative council, with each zone running functions pertaining to intelligence, revenue, law and order, etc. Pakistan has done well to preserve and augment the lineage of the most regressive, militant, and medieval-minded tyranny in the history of the post-modern world. The US of course has provided financial and moral endorsements, among other things. Pakistani popular demand these days includes shoving the ISI twin babies of the Haqqani Network and the Hizb e Islami into the Afghanistan peace settlement table.

The bottom line is that there is no solution in Afghanistan without Pakistani consultation, intervention, or approval. Even if there is, Washington does not want to consider it. It is absolutely mind-boggling to think about the status: the Rogue being consulted by Gluttony, to decide the fate of the Clueless. Or is it? Recent developments suggest that the Glutton is trying to outsmart the Rogue by holding secret talks with the Talibs in the presence (and absence, depending on whether its sunny or windy outside) of the President of the Clueless [atimes.com].

In the middle of it all, whenever they are free, the Pakistan Taliban kill Pakistani troops and broadcast messages about getting closer to possessing the nuclear arsenal, to help the Pakistani establishment demonstrate its helplessness to the rest of the world. (They do not bother about managing US perceptions anymore—it is a done deal). These are specially orchestrated undertakings, threatening to take Pakistan near the threshold of a civil war, scare the wits out of the reasonably functional governments of the Middle East and south Asia, and bring it back before long. So much ado!

* * * *

For the TAPI to successfully get operational, the obligation would be on each of the transit countries to secure the pipeline. Part of the Afghan stretch will be buried underground as a safeguard against attacks. The local war lords will probably be paid to guard it. But Kabul knows that they cannot be trusted, and naturally it expects NATO to provide security. And that necessitates a long-term US military presence in Afghanistan. The US can now be seen running around busily kissing everyone representing every colour—the Uzbek, Tajik, Hazara, and other northern Afghan Warlords, the "good" Taliban of southern Afghanistan, the Pakistani trio of government-military-ISI—in, out, cross-border everywhere. Well, the people there love to kiss and be kissed, so I understand. But for the US, the TAPI is the prize—greed glorified. The only people who miss being kissed in this whole bargain are the poverty-ridden general population of Afghanistan and Pakistan. It cannot be helped.

I am left with two thoughts:

a) This oil/gas saga is like a quintessential Bollywood award function. The same names and faces keep turning up, get nominated year after year, keep sharing the same old PJs on stage, while the same audience pretends to laugh; and

b) The ghost of Saddam must be wondering why on earth he got slapped when everyone and his neighbour were stealing.

7 Islamic Fundamentalism — *The 2nd Protection Racket*

Now I know why you wanna hate me...
Coz hate is all the world has ever seen lately!

    —Limp Bizkit, *Take a Look Around*

The King called up his jet fighters
He said you better earn your pay
Drop your bombs between the Minarets
Down the Casbah way

    —The Clash, *Rock the Casbah*

"Jihad" is an oft-used word. Most people, Muslims or not, have heard this term a number of times in their life, and even those dwelling at the remotest corners of the globe have surely noticed this word through newspaper, radio, or TV reports after 9/11. The usage pattern of this word in the West-dominated mainstream media is roughly like this: Not all Islamic religious or political movements are called Jihad. The Tunisian and Egyptian popular revolutions that overthrew their ruling governments were not referred to as Jihads, for example. Jihad is only used when describing some form of Islamic extremism against the West. This tendency to use and oftentimes abuse the word 'Jihad' for the want of a better expression most of the times, when it comes to registering Islamic agitation against the West in general or in particular is not correct. But we do it nonetheless. There are three reasons behind it. The first and most important reason is that the religious group that is behind a particular act of violence usually proclaims through some media outlet that it is their jihad against the West. Naturally, the media uses the term to identify and classify a series of similar actions or reactions—a tag always helps. And third, over-usage of this word subtly antagonises the already-prejudiced non-Muslims at large against Muslims in general.

It is important to comprehend what is normally understood by this expression.

Jihad is correctly defined as the struggle against oppression, against anything deemed unethical. The root of the struggle is identified as the effort. I promise not to bring too much history into this discussion and to try to keep it very brief. Mohammed distinguished two forms of Jihad—the greater one, against evils within oneself, and the lesser one, against another [islamanswers.net]. Practically however, the word has an infinite amount of complexity around it, as thinkers and scholars across religions have debated the legitimacy of its aspects. In different references in the Koran, the doctrine of jihad has been used differently. In the beginning, when Islam was unpopular in the Arabian peninsula, jihad was deemed to be a defensive form of struggle. During the later stages, when Mohammed triumphed, jihad gradually found an offensive connotation through his preaching and the wars he waged.

What we typically see among beleaguered Muslim communities today is their individual interpretation of the doctrine to advance their causes. Among other things pertaining to the West, the only banner that unites such a perception is that the West has never abandoned their Crusade, so naturally jihad should not be abandoned either. The struggle is characterised by its timelessness. "We believe that we are still at the beginning of the war... it is a path that the Muslims have to walk upon until the judgement day" said Suleiman Abu Ghaith, spokesperson for bin Laden, in early 2002 [Burke, *Al Qaeda*, 33]. After such remarks, to blame the Western media unequivocally in respect of usage of the word jihad would be naïve. Of course a few other words and phrases are used carelessly: Islamism, Islamic radicalism, Islamic fundamentalism, extremism, etc. Whatever it is called, putting the real or perceived parameters of such words aside, jihad today can be viewed as Islamic socio-political evolution in response to Western dominance; essentially reactionary in nature.

The Idea of a Second Scapegoat
From the point of view of the brokers of globalisation there was a job to do after the fall of the Berlin Wall and the disintegration of the USSR. When the "evil" of the twentieth century officially died, there was a

pressing need to build another suitable scapegoat. South and Latin America, influenced by proximity to home, reason, flexibility, lack of will, or whatever, did not look promising or realistic enough to be propelled into satanic status; simply speaking, they were not good dartboard candidates. Ditto for a large part of Asia: with nations like Singapore, South Korea, the Philippines, Taiwan, etc, already marching under the same house-flag that the Triad (USA, western Europe, Japan) was waving. In the 1990s, the Non-Aligned Movement was passé. Africa was weak and disintegrating as always. That left the Islam-influenced Middle East—one unit (of geography/ religion/ people) strong enough to sustain the massive amount of pressure that usually followed with US "interest," and spirited enough in their ignorance to possibly save western faces during the eventual need of a dartboard. A new chapter therefore began towards the end of the twentieth century, where religious differences and other showcased shortcomings costumed the Muslims of the Middle East in the role of the new punching bag for western policy makers. It was a status that was a heady mixture of intervention and retaliation; a classic Newton's-Third-Law tuned to perfection. Of course, most of the actions remained camouflaged from citizens at large, only the reactions were discussed, dissected, judged, archived, and revived time and again to keep people under the all-good-is-us-and-all-bad-are-them impression—that exercise was a re-run of the past.

Things were generally well-balanced to begin with. The West experienced an unprecedented decade of prosperity. The US controlled nearly all the global resources and transnational corporations romped freely around the planet, the Russian pulse was barely registering on the monitor, and the citizens were blissfully ignorant as always. They thought they had everything covered. And that was when 9/11 happened. Out of other messages that this incident conveyed to the West, one grabbed its public by the collar: if you thought you were safe and away—think again.

The Equation. . .

. . . Has always been rife with mutual distrust and no one has ever initiated a reconciliation. In the West, Islam is often equated with fundamentalism. In Islamic culture, the West is always the oppressor. I wonder which perception preceded which. And once one binds oneself with that as an analytical tool, it becomes difficult to see beyond it. Islam draws on a deep historic antipathy towards the West that grew during the Middle Ages' Crusades, and later during the carving up of the Ottoman Empire and the subsequent secret Skyes-Picot Agreement that was to divide Arabia for the benefit of the British and Americans. The Western mindset is clearly reflected through Western history that highlights the lone Crusade that the Muslims won against the Christian marauders as an episode that should never be forgotten or allowed to be repeated. The West identifies Muslims as "constricted, anti-modern, anti-secular, anti-democratic, anti-globalisation, anti-Semitic, anti-emancipation, anti-feminist, anti-plural, and consisting of followers enthralled by the promise of revolution that would put Islam in charge of the state again." The Muslims identify the West as an immoral and savage culture that has been historically exploiting their natural resources for self-development purposes. While the "promise of revolution" in Muslim expectations has put Islamic fundamentalism on an "inevitable crash course with secularism" in the minds of the western population, it has also taken special care to obliterate those Islamic movements and people with a bent towards rational self-determination [Milton-Edwards, *Islamic Fundamentalism since 1945*, 3–4]. With such a tipping-point ready, who needed a reason to panic?

The Post-Communism Demon

Out of the thousands of young recruits that trekked into Afghanistan between 1996 and 2001 to be trained in the al Qaeda camps, you may be surprised to learn that Osama bin Laden did not kidnap or brainwash a single one into his cause of global jihad. Neither did he retain anyone against his will in the camps. Staying was completely voluntary. Most of the young men were dedicated to the cause beforehand; they wanted to commit their lives and faculties to this most extreme form of Islamic militancy.

Similarly, roughly during the same time, al Qaeda is said to have been flooded with multiple requests—for money, expertise, logistics, etc—that came from virtually every corner of the world. The intended use of the requested units were mostly destructive: bombs and mass murders. Journalist, observer, and writer Jason Burke expresses that it was a time of sharing in the ideas of al Qaeda, of subscribing to the al Qaeda worldview, but without a tangible connection. And as a matter of fact, al Qaeda as a physical unit would soon cease to exist due to military interventions. The idea however would not only remain intact, but actually spread among the minds of millions of people [Burke, *Al Qaeda*, 13–14].

Islamic extremism has not slowed down or dissipated—it has just decentralised and become more fluid. The myriad groups, often of only two or three members, are not controlled by a single head. They are self-fueled. The al Qaeda maxim, along with Western interventionism, has ushered in an era of liquid Jihad that no government or state can control or contain by conventional methods. This increase in the threat and a reduced power to counter or mitigate it on the part of the affluent nations has had far-reaching effects. Some were visible almost immediately during the ten years after 1996, and more will become visible in the future.

The Facilitating Factors

Islam as a legacy of Mohammed has been fraught with ignorance and intolerance, betrayal, and personalised agendas ever since his death. Most of the early Caliphs were murdered sometime or the other. There was a schism on whom to appoint and follow, right after Mohammed's death, which gave birth to the Shia-Sunni division, the fall-out of which continues even today. Shia Iran or Bahrain, al Hasa in Saudi Arabia or Shia minorities in different patches in the Middle East—notably Iraq during Saddam's rule—have been subjected to some of the worst Sunni-inflicted traumas of recent times through terrorist bombings and mass murders. All religions have basic splits in them, but genocides stopped many years ago. With Islam the story continues.

This history of intolerance however, has not been wholly organic. Between the early turmoil and the strife that we experience today, there have been notable phases of inclusivity, farsightedness, and forbearance. During Europe's Dark Ages, the Muslim world recovered, preserved, and built upon the learning of the ancients both east and west, and integrated them into the mathematics and experimental science that probably made the modern world possible. While Europe massacred its Jews, the Muslims of the Middle East fostered them, as well as some of the earliest

Christian settlements that are still in existence today. Compared to the religious and factional wars that ripped Europe, killing off huge swathes of its population in the centuries between the Christian Reformation and World War II, the Muslim world saw relatively minor conflicts.

The dormant behavioural-fanaticism was regenerated and nudged to occupy the centre stage during European Colonialism, especially British. The result has been the inclusion of a major concern in addition to the already existing Shia-Sunni issue. The British, siding first with Ibn Saud of Arabia to finish off the Ottoman Empire following their policy of divide and rule; later, by deliberately muddling the Israel-Palestine affair during their withdrawal; finally the US in its greed for global resources has managed to further the split across a different plane. Today we have an incredible number of Muslims who are intolerant towards the rest of the world—especially the West.

Islam, though historically hailed to be the pioneer in many areas of art, architecture, and science has also had a mostly blinkered and vastly illiterate general population. Notable exceptions are to be found in the Plains of Bengal, but such examples are limited. Their concepts of elemental things like society or community, or more complex issues like liberty or democracy, have always been handicapped. This void has traditionally been occupied by a zest for religion, and that in turn has historically been misused by a handful of clerics mostly for driving their personal agenda—we are probably witnessing the crest of it since the 1980s. Today, whether it is a disdain for anything deemed un-Islamic that has led to intolerance towards liberty or plurality or whether instead a lack of knowledge or the will to understand these processes and complexities has led to intolerance and a more fervent desire to simplify things by clinging to their cultural roots is a topic for debate, but the end result is the same.

This is not to say that other civilizations have been flawless in conduct or seamless in transition. There have been extremely dirty cases in the history of every civilization that we have known of, but the difference lies in that they have progressed, albeit bumpily. In more modern times, the ideologies or operative philosophies may have been eastern or western, but in the end they have mostly resulted in more tolerance, fewer killings, more flexibility in thoughts or action, marked increases in basic awareness, more social concern and plurality, and so on. But in the case of the Islamic countries, with the notable exceptions of Indonesia or Jordan, social progress has been extremely slow or nonexistent. The West, first in their Imperialistic ambitions, and later in their need for a fall-guy, worked on these two primary shortcomings.

Wahhabism: The Beginning of Modern Islam

Nearly two hundred years ago the al-Saud clan of the Arabian peninsula gave refuge to a militant Islamic preacher called Mohammed ibn Abd al-Wahhab. This man's radical doctrines gradually came to be known as Wahhabism, and it took the Muslim world by storm during the 1800s. It held to the original interpretation of the divine message as revealed to Mohammed—the rigid, thousand-year-old version. The followers of al Wahhab were known as Wahhabi, and there was a breed of fighters among them who were known as the Ikhwan. They believed that they were fighting for the cause of Allah, and that their death would make them martyrs and grant them a visa for heaven. This made them extremely effective fighters. The Ikhwan were used many times over, for many causes both personal and social, by Wahhab and by the al Saud clan chieftains [Burke, *Al Qaeda*, 42–43].

The Wahhabi cause was ardently supported by Saudi rulers. They used the Ikhwan brutes to enforce their school of thought. In the early 1800s, after "cleansing" Mecca and Medina, then under Ottoman rule, they clashed with the Ottoman empire itself. The decaying empire however was still potent enough to teach the upstart Saudi clan a lesson. With the help of the Pasha of Egypt the Ottomans thrashed the Wahhabi forces, as a result of which the doctrine went underground. But it managed to survive.

According to historian and Orientalist Bernard Lewis, the second alliance of Wahhabi doctrine and Saudi force began in the last years of the Ottoman Empire and it has continued to the present day. This was achieved and consolidated largely by the British, who were lining up allies against the Ottoman-German alliance during World War I. They signed an agreement with Ibn Saud to legitimise his independence and his kingdom in 1915, thereby forming a strategic alliance against the Ottomans in the Arabian Peninsula.

Following the War, with more British-orchestrated annexations, Ibn Saud proclaimed himself King of Hijaz and Sultan of Najd and its dependencies in 1926. This was immediately recognised by the European powers. There was a markedly slower pace of recognition among the Islamic countries. Egypt was among the slowest.

Two significant things happened shortly after 1926. Grateful for allied support, the Saudi minister of finance signed a deal with Standard Oil of California. That was the beginning of a petro-dollar-based financial foundation. The year was 1933. The second thing was a tribute to the Wahhabi-Saud friendship. King Abdul Aziz allowed the *ulama* (Muslim religious scholars) to put their noses into everything, from government to the bureaucracy, madrassas, and NGOs, and even traveled the extra mile to establish outfits to promote Wahabbism internationally. This marked the beginning of many present-day problems.

The Sauds quickly became immensely rich and powerful. This in turn had an impact on the world of Islam. With official backing, Wahhabism, which was the state-enforced doctrine of the custodians of two of the holiest places of Islam—found itself sitting on immense wealth, both tangible and otherwise. Indoctrination centres opened up across the world that taught the most intolerant version of the religion. These largely went unnoticed because secular governments seldom interfered in religious curricula, and because to western powers during the period leading up to World War II and the Cold War, religious extremism was not the enemy; communism was.

The Muslim Brotherhood and Political Islamism
At the end of the World War I the European side of the defeated Ottoman Empire saw the ascent to power of a Young Turk named Kemal Ataturk, who would later become the leader of Turkey. An Army officer, Ataturk, in his zeal to secularise the society, abolished the Ottoman Caliphate and implemented a series of brutalities on the general population in an effort to modernise them.

People across societies and religions have always been trying to find answers to problems that they think plague their societies. Al Wahhab sought answers and so did Osama bin Laden. Likewise, in the year 1928 a small movement called the Muslim Brotherhood was started by Hassan al Banna in Egypt. Known as the father of modern political Islamism, al Banna, like so many other thinkers before him, sought answers. The ban of the Ottoman Caliphate, the carving-up of the Middle East (by the Skyes-Picot Agreement), and the forcible secularization of society, which is taboo among followers of Islam, were perceived as a humiliation and an existential threat in the minds of many Muslims. Al Banna believed wholeheartedly in the Prophet's teachings and messages. But what confronted him was an unequal society. That led him to believe that the ulama had failed, and that jihad was the key.

But al Banna was not your modern-day Kalashnikov-totting maniac. He was an intelligent man, whose idea of jihad involved "literacy, education, social services, and justice" [Burke, *Al Qaeda*, 48]. That was the logic behind the movement called Muslim Brotherhood. Al Banna hoped to achieve results in this jihad of his, through preaching. He sought to transform his society at its core over time. He recruited from every section of the society, built schools and colleges, and founded hospitals and clinics. In twenty years Muslim Brotherhood was a formidable philanthropic force, with a strong political presence in Egypt. Al Banna represented the cerebral side of political Islamism—that of proceeding towards the desired goal by social activism through what one could possibly call a peaceful jihad, and that was what the first generation of political Islam in the 20th century sounded like. But the Egyptian secret police would soon assassinate al Banna just after dissolving his group for manifesting shades of communism. Unfortunately, his death marked the end of the course of peaceful jihad.

Addition of Hues

Syed Qutb, another Egyptian, a school inspector, joined the Muslim Brotherhood sometime during his late forties. He was from the lower middle class but had a literate background. He was frail, a bachelor for life, and a radical whose rise to prominence lay in his prolific messages. But Egypt during those days was trying hard to fall in line with the West by promoting secularism, so Qutb was arrested. From prison he composed his most influential work, Milestones, that is often dubbed "Islam's Communist Manifesto." What corresponded in his messages to what al Banna thought or expressed was that Islam had been corrupted by outside interference. But what was different was the acknowledgment that the corruption was not restricted to the outsiders—even insiders were corrupted. Continuous repression of Islamic religious expression by Egypt and Turkey, and their apparent urge to westernise, possibly led him to think so. What was also different between him and al Banna was that al Banna believed in gradual social activism and a peaceful, constructive, and all-encompassing jihad. But Syed Qutb believed in radicalism. He would be hanged in 1966, but not before incorporating hues of radical ideologies into modern political Islam.

During the time of al Banna but separated from it by geography and distance, the Indian subcontinent witnessed the rise of a religious activist of a different kind. He would rise to become one of the foremost advocates of the "theory of distance"—that of keeping non-believers as far as possible from Allah's chosen ones. He would later migrate to Pakistan after the 1947 separation and wage his campaign against all infidels, apostates, and heresies. His name was Maulana Sayyid Abdul Ala Maududi, and while Muhammad Ali Jinnah was the "father" of Pakistan, author MJ Akbar with proper justification has called Maududi the "Godfather of Pakistan." This man would go on to create the far-right Islamist political party *Jamaat e Islami*, and infuse radicalism into political Islam. He would later defame a deceased Muhammad Ali Jinnah and crush his sapling of a legacy by luring the new-born and would-be-secular Pakistan into the folds of a medievalist outlook; he also would infuse in the Pakistani establishment and elites a virulent form of radicalism that would later shape Pakistan's destiny. And among many other things, he would map "a path for conversion of Pakistan into an Islamic state" and even planned to introduce "Islamic Sciences" based on a "revised history" [M J Akbar, *Tinderbox*]. Maulana Maududi's ideas put a fresh coat of win-lose radicalism on the 20th century Asian and Middle Eastern Muslim psyche that would influence people, events, and the shape of the modern world.

The Tracks That Emerged

Perhaps the best modern examples of religious extremism and political Islam can by drawn from the Saudi-sponsored-Pakistan-bolstered Sunni militancy of the 1970s, 80s, and 90s (most notably in the Afghan War)—

the subsequent emergence of al Qaeda and the Taliban at one end of southwest Asia; and the rise of Shia Hezbollah in Lebanon at the other end . Although there are other significant political groups like Hamas in Palestine or the erstwhile Jammu and Kashmir Liberation Front in Pakistan, when it comes to al Qaeda, the Taliban, and Hezbollah, their origins (both Shia and Sunni sects), the scale of their operations, and the level of their engagement with different international peacekeeping agencies amply explains the tracks that emerged.

The Saudi-Sponsored Sunni Militancy

The Iranian revolution of 1979 that propelled Ayatollah Khomeni into prominence alarmed the Wahhabi Saudis into a frenzied action. A revolution in Iran meant two things. Shia popularity and/or dominance in the adjoining areas, and the fact of religion presenting itself as an ideology powerful enough to overthrow tyrannical kings and establish a new economic order. Earlier, "Riyadh had always invoked Islam to uphold the political status quo." But Iran changed that. The Shia strand of Islamism, which was historically a minority in the Islamic world, suddenly assumed the status of "the world's most radical and inspiring example of modern Muslim activism." This was a new situation. It had the potential to establish some positive uniformity in the otherwise severely poor and illiterate Middle East population. To prevent this, Saudi Arabia followed the example of the Egyptian government's treatment of the Muslim Brotherhood. But Iran was a different country and outside the scope of direct intervention, so proxies were let loose. The government of Saudi Arabia, with the support of Western powers that had vested interests, started pumping its oil money into promoting hardcore Sunni Islamism. "The result was the exporting on an industrial scale of Wahhabi, Salafi, neo-traditionalist, or 'hard' Islam. . . with almost obsessive emphasis on outward details of Islamic practices, Quranic literalism, and profound hostility to all other forms of Islamic practice, let alone other religions" wherever possible. The financing was further bolstered by states like the UAE and Kuwait—two other long standing allies of the United States [Burke, *Al Qaeda*, 60].

The Saudi and allied financial and ideological help particularly affected the fate of Afghanistan, both during their war against the Soviet

Union and afterwards. The period of war saw an incredible influx of tribes from all over the Muslim world, all coming to fight as Mujahideens in what was known as the Afghan resistance. Already in line were the numerous domestic tribal communities of Afghanistan—the idea of an armed resistance against what was deemed an evil Western power was the hot favourite. Money was everywhere. The CIA pumped in money and weapons, routed through Pakistan's ISI, which retained full control of the affair. The Saudis matched whatever amount the Americans poured in. In those days though there was an element of preference in terms of alignment of radical thoughts on the part of the tribes and militant outfits with whatever ideas the Pakistani ISI subscribed to; even then, many insignificant groups were also sponsored. People could open Mujahideen groups out of nothing, if they had access to money and arms. The most notable of these was Sayyaf's outfit, the Islamic Dawah Organization of Afghanistan (*Ittehad e Islami*).

It was during this time that radical Islamic political and philosophical ideas underwent profound transformations. One of the chief reasons behind this was a man named Abdul Azzam. A Palestinian and a member of the Muslim Brotherhood who was settled in Islamabad, Pakistan, Azzam was not then an original thinker like Qutb or al Banna, "but he was a powerful orator who fused the historic and the contemporary to create something of unprecedented power." For him, the jihad in Afghanistan was a physical, moral, and religious mandate for all Muslims—"the sixth pillar of faith", and he clearly indicated that the jihad had to spread everywhere: Palestine, Bokhara, Lebanon, Chad, Eritrea, Somalia, the Philippines, Burma, southern Yemen, Tashkent, and even Andalusia. This kind of idea is bound to strike a chord in many places. Little wonder that he became incredibly popular, a major influence even in Osama bin Laden's life. But Azzam was more than that. He instilled the desire for martyrdom among a large number of illiterate volunteers, "quoting the single *hadith* in which the Prophet assures the *shahid* absolution from all sins, seventy-two beautiful virgins, and permission to bring seventy members of their household into Paradise with them." In addition he compiled a book of some implausible eyewitness accounts of dead Mujahideens, complete with angels and the works. He was the modern-day exaggeration of Maulana Maududi of *Jamat e Islami*. His teachings, his language, his innovative stories were to become the backbone of the new wave of Islamic resistance that was gradually taking shape [Burke, *Al Qaeda*, 72–75].

The initial phase of the Arab-Afghan movement saw people with some academic or technical background leading from the front. With time, the illiterates filled the landscape. They were typically ignorant of the cultural or intellectual legacy of political Islam and the background that preceded them. For them cheap symbolism and the allegories of Azzam made more sense. The coherence of al Banna gradually faded as Abdul Azzam and his like took over the reins of modern Islamism. With some more time, the Egyptian brains and intellectual angle was gone, and by the end the Afghan resistance movement was a hardened version of more black and white radicalism along the lines of the Pakistani psyche as developed by Maulana Maududi, and far removed from the worldview of the early Muslim Brotherhood. It was constructed from the "rigorous Salafi reformism of the Wahhabis, from Azzam's call of martyrdom in a pan-Islamic international jihad against oppression, from the very real experience of the brutal violence and chaos of modern warfare and from the empowering confidence founded in the belief, however wrong, that Islam alone had defeated the Soviets. . .." This impression that it was Islam's victory that defeated the USSR led to a feeling of invincibility among them. "The culture and sophistication of the *Umayyads* and the *Abbasids*, the architecture and poetry, the philosophy and the lore of the Muslim world were rejected as tainted by weakness and corrupted by failure." In Afghanistan, the ideology underwent a metamorphosis into degradation—and when the Afghan war was over, the containment phase got over too. This modernised version was to branch out and spread elsewhere [Burke, *Al Qaeda*, 83].

Pakistan, a key ally of the US in this part of the globe, played a pivotal role during the Soviet occupation. The state had unprecedented access to US money and munitions, and, logistics notwithstanding, it also had a role in human resources pertaining to recruitment, indoctrination, and training of Mujahideens. After the war was over the recruitment continued chiefly for continuing insurgency and infiltration in Kashmir. Again, many of the new recruits also made inroads into the then-new al Qaeda whose chief ambition was to continue jihad outside of Afghanistan. The chief patron, Osama bin Laden, wanted to bring about Islamic revolution to the countries of the *Ummah*. The key strategy was remarkable. For the first time, here was a group that was striving to capitalise on the international alliances of different fundamentalist outfits made during the Afghan war, by threading them through a common foundation. If Azzam denoted degraded modernity, al Qaeda was to usher in the liquid version of it.

If anyone could claim a prize for introducing yet another mutant strain of degraded Islamism, it would be Pakistan, again. From the more gradualist secularism of Muhammad Ali Jinnah to Pakistan's state obsession with Maulana Maududi's vision, the single-minded fixation on drawing favours from Saudi Arabia, a passionate hatred towards India and utter disregard towards social or economic governance—these eventually gave rise to an extreme right-wing, radical, neo-con variety of Islamism called Deobandism. This called for rejecting politics altogether, promoted worshipping of the clergy, and recognised their monopoly on the interpretation of the holy book. This strain was not new, being formulated during the mid nineteenth century in the then-undivided subcontinent. To counter what was perceived as the Hindu "superiority" threat, the Muslims thought of preserving their identity through literal observance of the Quran and the Hadiths. As we have seen, this reaction was to be repeated often in the future. To preserve their identity and thus escalate superiority, a network of Madrassas was created where the young were taught the literal interpretation of the texts. Gradually, the madrassas became "an isolated 'Islamicised space' and their inhabitants became an idealised 'Islamic society'" [Burke, *Al Qaeda*, 92–93]. These students were known as the Talibans. By 1967, Pakistan had around 1000 such indoctrination centres running mostly in the stone-illiterate and ignorant Pakhtun regions along the North West frontier. By 1988, some 400,000 students were educated through them. Because Deobandi was so like Saudi Wahhabism, and because the government-run schools in Pakistan were perpetually lacking funds, money for their support came from the Gulf states and these madrassas became a huge hit in little time—and were to play a major role in Afghanistan shortly.

When Mullah Omar surfaced on the radar during 1994, his small Taliban outfit was a thing of beauty in the eyes of the Pakistani establishment. A grip on Afghanistan meant "strategic depth" over India, a possible actualization of the Trans-Afghan Pipeline, an opening of routes for trade with the central Asian states, and, interestingly, a clear upper hand in opium and drug smuggling; Afghanistan is the largest supplier of opium in the world. Pakistan was the first country to recognise the Taliban government of Afghanistan, naturally.

Hezbollah

A small group of ill-equipped guerrillas when they began, Hezbollah gained international notoriety by its involvement in the kidnapping of over eighty Westerners throughout the 1980s, for the attack on the US embassy in Beirut in 1983 that killed sixty three people, for the bombing of the US Marines' barracks in Beirut in October that same year, for the deaths of twenty nine people in the 1992 bombing of the Israeli embassy in Argentina, and for the death of a hundred more in the 1994 attack on a Jewish cultural centre in London. At the same time, domestic interest in the party grew phenomenally in Lebanon due to its eighteen-year struggle against Israeli occupation forces in South Lebanon, and its triumph over Israel in 2000.

The emergence of such a rare breed in the realms of radical Islamism was not only because of the Israeli invasion of Lebanon, or a continued Western intervention as we know, but surprisingly also because of the will to upgrade the living conditions of the Lebanese Shi'ite community, as progressive analysts of the region opine. Historically deprived and extremely poor, the Shi'ite community was almost like a third world within Lebanon. Their sporadic emigration to the capital of Beirut led only to further miseries that came along with settlement within urban slums. They were the most disadvantaged segment of Lebanese society compared to the affluent Christian and Sunni counterparts, and were under-represented in Parliament, civil services, and government. The situation was ideal for religious revival to give rise to a burgeoning radical, neo-con attitude, as we have seen fairly regularly in Islam's case, but Hezbollah was a marked exception. "The roots of Shi'ite political mobilisation, and hence the formation of Hezbollah, lie in the community's radicalisation by Arab nationalist, socialist, and communist organisations," says Amal Saad-Ghorayeb. He goes on to register emphatically that "the communal politicisation of the Shi'ites preceded their religious politicisation" [Saad-Ghorayeb, *Hizbu'llah: Politics and Religion*, 1–15].

And it gets more surprising. If we follow Hezbollah's philosophy, we find some remarkable deviations, something that talks in a language that most of us are acquainted with. For example, they strive for an Islamic state, but, at the same time they are matured enough to indefinitely postpone this due to the present socio-political shortcomings. Their political logic centres on the oppressed-oppressor theory, but unlike most of the Sunni-Salafi jihadist outfits, there are no religious shades to it. An oppressed person to them need not be a Muslim, but anyone who is "socially and economically deprived, politically oppressed and culturally repressed." Their theory of political action is humanitarian; the party does not equate secularism with oppression or sin like the Salafi, Deobandi, and Sunni religious groups. They are realistic in their approach towards governance too. Unlike Sunni outfits that dream about a Golden Age that they seek to recreate, Hezbollah does not hold such a delusion. Also, they are honest with affairs of the state. "Both the party's admirers and detractors agree that, of all the political forces in Lebanon, Hizbu'llah is the only political party which has not been tainted by charges of corruption or political opportunism and which has resolutely stuck to its principles" [Saad-Ghorayeb, *Hizbu'llah: Politics and Religion*, 1–15].

The reason behind the development of more prominent strains of Islamization within Hezbollah is said to be the result of the Israeli invasion of 1982 [Saad-Ghorayeb, *Hizbu'llah: Politics and Religion*, 1–15]. Though radicalism was clearly there during the first war of 1978, the integration of radicalism happened during the second war when various Shi'ite Islamic groups joined under the banner of the newly born Hezbollah. But despite that, this military-political movement uniquely bound together by intellectual, religious, and political lines has progressed to become the largest parliamentary block in the country. Despite some apprehension among the marginalised Christians of Lebanon, Hezbollah continues to earn a huge amount of respect from them. From bombings and assassinations, the group has traveled a long way in a very short time.

When I was a child snippets of the Lebanon Civil War on TV were an everyday affair, and Hezbollah used to be the most dreaded word on the screen. Today, in terms of assimilation, especially in relation to the Saudi- Pakistani sponsored Sunni militancy, a section of prominent post-modern thinkers are of the opinion that "suddenly, al Qaeda had become a minor player in the Salafi-jihadist constellation and even a minor player among the 1.5 billion *umma* in terms of how to fight back against the hegemony of the West," as Hezbollah and a larger Shi'ite resistance movement enjoyed unprecedented support compared to the "cultish, isolated bunch of Salafi-jihadists. What is also notable is that in Egypt and in Jordan the Sunni Muslim Brotherhood—the oldest, largest modern Islamist movement in the world—supported Hezbollah unconditionally. That meant it was supporting Hezbollah's patron the Islamic Republic of Iran as well— this Sunni-Shiite convergence illustrating an overwhelming Shiite prestige revival much to the chagrin of Salafi-jihadists and the House of Saud" [Escobar, *Globalistan*, 102].

The Future

Hezbollah is much-hated among the policy makers of the West, for a number of reasons. This is not your average maniacal brutal Islamist outfit anymore. This organization has lately demonstrated an all-inclusive, pan-religious, pan-ethnic approach towards development of their nation. Hezbollah incredibly has revived the political Islamism of al Banna. And for genuine reasons, this organization has now been accepted and legitimised in Lebanon. What is more, Hezbollah and its patron Nasrallah (the new Nasser, as he is called) are now the current international role-model among the vast majority of moderate Muslims spanning the globe for how to resist the Western greed system.

There can be nothing more frustrating than when a puppet breaks the strings.

The idea behind continuously agitating Muslim populations or Islamic nations of the world was to create/recreate the Wahhabi magic or the Deobandi charm, and promote Islamophobia among the non-Muslims—you know, the same tack that the West took during the Cold War era. The act began impressively too. Extremist groups in Africa, the Middle East, and the Mediterranean region blowing up buildings, hijacking planes, and kidnapping people, border tensions in Kashmir and Israel, the Afghan war and the birth of the Mujahideens, civil war in Lebanon—it was a damn good start. But gradually things began to change. Hezbollah is the best example. Hamas in Palestine and a re-emerging Iran can be two more. While the revolutions in Tunisia or Egypt are too new and a lot remains to be seen, at least they have been for the cause of democracy, not for a Wahhabi-style "return to the golden age" dream. While the UAE and Saudi Arabia are still holding onto the coat-tails of Uncle Sam and his grand design of Islamophobia, there has been an incredible amount of change happening in the recent past. The population of nations like Turkmenistan do not hold on too strongly to religion, because of a Soviet past. They drink vodka too. Iran or Lebanon do not subscribe to the Sunni-Salafi-Jihadi concept. Turkey has integrated with the EU. Morocco has not, but culturally it is almost like an extension of Mediterranean Europe. Egypt, Tunisia, or Bahrain have either gone their own way in trying to democratise the affairs of their state or are fighting to do so. Saudi Arabia is trying its best to stop this nightmare wherever possible, for example by sending troops to Bahrain—something that promises to be increasingly difficult with time.

It appears as if a lot of people these days can see through contrived Islamophobia. I know it is difficult to do so from everywhere, for instance from India—we are neighbours to Pakistan after all—but that does not change the fact. And this very fact can be a reason for renewed Triad efforts to rehash the Islamic threat. Al Qaeda is a perfect candidate for that.

Things have not changed much after the death of bin Laden, as the very concept of jihad that got liquified during his time has traveled more already. At the other end, Afghanistan poses many serious challenges—something that will continue during the next decade or so. Iraq has been seriously damaged and no efforts are being made on the part of the desta-bilizing forces to restore it. On the contrary, fresh efforts are being made to further destabilise the country by pitching the Northern Kurds against the ruling al Maliki government. The Long War is gradually extend-ing its tentacles towards northern Africa. The immediate effect of these is a steep increase in an already prevalent anti-Western sentiment. The Middle East is still extremely poor. (You can get e-mail attachments of gold-and-silver plated Audi convertibles of the different Sheikhs or Emirs—that does not change a thing). Exploitation is rife and the general population is illiterate. The wish to retaliate is extremely strong. The catalysts too, are in place. Saudi Arabia is still the global sponsor of Wahhabism and Pakistan is still the global "human resources" manager for Salafi terrorists. And while political parties like Hezbollah put in efforts to address their domestic issues, outside of Lebanon or Palestine millions of others who do not have a Hamas or a Hezbollah to look after them are left with the likes of the late Osama bin Laden or Ayman al Zawahiri and their rhetoric of universal Islamic *ulema*. They probably do not register that this is a once-upon-a-time friend of the CIA. Who knows? Maybe, just maybe, a successful accomplishment of 9/11 did legitimise George Bush junior's rule after all, while the Military-Industrial Complex got a fresh lease of life as havoc was wreaked on the Middle East. Or maybe they do register these facts but do not currently have many options.

The Road to Acceptance
Even though the affairs pertaining to Islam sound confusingly complex as of now, the good thing is that there is some semblance of order, of sanity somewhere. It has been acknowledged that the concept of jihad has liquefied and has become extremely mobile. The result has been an unprecedented growth in surveillance societies and stepped up military spending across developed nations to aid the Greed System of transnational corporations—there is a tentative feeling that things will progress. The recent popular domestic revolutions in parts of North Africa are a testimony to that. Though the US and NATO characteristically keep playing the old game of selectively supporting anti-government forces in Libya or Syria on the one hand and pro-monarchical forces in Bahrain on the other, the regime changes so far have not actually resulted in changes in governance style. (Egypt at this writing is still ruled by a committee of commanders once faithful to Mubarak.) Although a broader rationale behind the US/NATO intervention is to control the Mediterranean Sea or encircle Iran, millions of us hope to witness that eureka moment in a near future when significant portions of the Middle East finally emerge, leaving perceived gains through religious extremism behind, and confirm a modernist approach to all-inclusive socio-political development.

Would it be through such movements or awareness campaigns that some group or person finally envisages and effects a path towards self determination through embracing modernist thinking? Would the awakening, of all places, be initiated in the Middle East? We do not yet know. But what we do know is that these days there is a good chance of an emergence of a class of activists, and if it happens in the Islamic world this set of people would hopefully be evolved enough to challenge the traditional clergies and monarchs and their negative effect on every form of society. They might, through natural succession, also be instrumental behind uncovering the hegemonic ambitions of the dominant powers like the KSA, the UAE and the plainly rogue establishments such as the ISI and Pakistani Army.

Not that there would not be any blowback. No one wants to give up control. But if the Muslim fraternity manages to brave that and rally behind their new reformists to push for a complete overhaul, only then would the world, among other things, finally say that Islam has stopped "cherry-picking" at modernization—"using science and technology but not the values that go with them, in order to achieve their political goal of new state forms based on a throwback to the past" [Milton-Edwards, *Islamic Fundamentalism since 1945*, 4].

Who knows, one of these days, we might just finally find the Eve who, despite the chauvinistic rules, could endure the onslaught.

8 The New World Order — *The Malady That Threatens*

For once the unthinkable happens, it becomes thinkable.
     —Immanuel Wallerstein

You can't say civilization don't advance... in every war they kill you in a new way.
     —Will Rogers

The G7 governments, under the able leadership of Washington, and the trio of the IMF, the World Bank, and the WTO, had introduced a nice racket during the phase we have come to call globalisation. The structural changes or so called economic "reforms" brought about some outlandish transformations in the globe. In no particular order, here they are:

Governments throughout the world were made to embrace a neo-liberal agenda under their watchful eyes, to the benefit of the transnational corporations. Even though this was called the "free" market system, it was controlled by the global conglomerates of politicians and capitalists. Since the underlying philosophy of these corporations was maximising profit, investments traveled across a borderless world, looking for the cheapest available labour, and settled wherever it found it. This resulted in the flight of capital and employment from a lot of countries. This led to the "internationalization of unemployment" soon afterwards [ilo.org]. Meanwhile, the countries that provided cheap labour competed to attract the transnationals. That resulted in less labour rights, deterioration of working conditions, and minimization of labour costs—the complete deregulation of labour laws, in other words.

In the face of the onslaught by the transnationals, the small or medium-sized businesses faced bad days. They either got bought out or went bankrupt. This heads-I-win-tails-you-lose situation had a few

147

distinct types of fallout. Mergers and acquisitions resulted in massive unemployment across industries. They also curbed the middle class entrepreneurial capacity. The resource, labour, and entrepreneurship that changed hands forcibly destroyed indigenous economies. They hit both the upper and lower middle class and pushed them further down, instead of lifting up the lowest strata.

All along, back in their homes the local population witnessed a restructuring in investment patterns. Capital investment in productive activities became a near-dead phenomenon. Financial speculation soon became the name of the game. Speculation and success in stock markets started underlining the economy. Needless to say, this was considered "outside of bona fide productive and commercial activities" [twnside.org]. Most people did not know about such hypotheses. This resulted in the rise of a minority of neo-billionaires, people who became rich through these financial games, at the cost of the rest of the society.

The underlying intent of this racket was to peacefully re-colonise the world by the calculated manipulation of local and international markets. What happened to countries that refused? Rules were made explicit, and examples were laid down. From Latin America towards the beginning of the twentieth century, two additional ones that acted as public memory refreshers were spread on the table—they were the Middle East twins of Iran and Iraq: one sanctioned to oblivion, another bombed out of the solar system. The world understood, at least temporarily.

They had a good thing going. Neo-Imperialists barging into a country wearing business suits, effecting structural adjustments, undoing state institutions, colluding with the leaders (capitalists) to commence repression, introducing a host of toys to make the urban population jump with joy at the marvels of liberalization—it was a pretty neat arrangement during a time that saw a manifold increase of global billionaires across all the triad nations; there was a marked increase in consumerism and a decrease in patriotism among global populations; the inebriated media clamoured for the wrong reasons—most of them belonged to the transnationals anyway. The icing on the cake was a bit of fear-motivation, infused into the system through Communism first and terrorism next, to keep things under control. Suddenly the financial bubble burst, the subprime crisis hit the United States, and bankers started jumping out of their high-rise windows.

* * * * *

Like the events of 9/11, the 2008 recession marked the beginning of many otherwise sleepy people's comprehension of the existence of some kind of a racket. But since an appreciation of logic among the global population on the whole remains weak, each individual or group drew conclusions in its own way. To further confuse things, interested governments stepped in with their perception management experts and muddled people's brains some more.

Economists, politicians, corporations, and governments now reluctantly include activists, social networking sites, bloggers, farmers, pastors, students, mullahs, and terrorists as fellow travelers in their journey through the twenty-first century. While that may not necessarily alter the profit sharing mechanism or destabilise the greed-system, the result is a fluid, chaotic and mostly intolerant group on their march through this new century. And since only a few nations and territories are critical to the affairs of the globe, this might be the right time to gauge their stance to try and understand the effect of the economic crisis on global society.

The United States of America (not again!)

In 1948 George Kennan said "We have about 50 percent of the world's wealth, but only 6.3 percent of its population." The idea was "to devise a pattern of relationships that will permit us to maintain this disparity" [Andrew Bacevich, *Why Military Spending is Untouchable*, counterpunch.org]. So much for promoting freedom and democracy, or seeking world peace. This programme was undertaken and at the end of World War II, much to the ecstasy of middle-class Americans, their Golden Age started. The effort has always been to try and follow Kennan's footsteps—then and now—to preserve this global superiority. That was sought through economic and military might, interventions, trade embargos—basically anything to force markets around the globe to yield to the US capital economy. During the early twenty-first century, the Bush Gang [Hamm, *Devastating Society*]. of neo-conservatives ravaged the length and breadth of the world during the time that they were in power. There was a hint that times were changing though, as all along American citizens wondered why bin Laden would want to attack them, why the US could not win the war in Iraq more easily, and why China prospers. They thought they were justified in their thinking, but then why were such incidents taking place? Then the 2008 recession happened. The house of cards came crashing down. The Bush Gang suddenly became the bad boys. Mr Obama cried "Yes, we can!" and millions of jobless Americans immediately voted him to power. They wanted him to finish the war in Afghanistan and Iraq—not because of the illegitimacy of it (the majority do not realise that it is illegitimate) but because they wanted to be safe, at the earliest. They wanted their jobs, those that got taken by South Asians, back. They demanded a return of their middle-class Golden Age.

For the world, there are two things to worry about: Triad greed, and the fallout from it. The advantage or disadvantage that comes with being a citizen of the US is that people there do not worry about either one. They think the US is not within the scope of the "rest of the world," so they can keep clear of the ill effects of globalisation. Not because it has not affected them, but because they earnestly do not believe that their government is capable of dishing out such treatment to them. They believe that all of this is a passing phase and will eventually be over and that America will again have Promised-Land status. This sounds like the Sunni pipe dream of returning to the Golden Age of Islam, and that is how it is; but with Americans, everything is justified. And of course one cannot fight and win against a fanatic's beliefs.

" 'Make poverty history!' A catchy slogan, and an admirable aim, it was adopted by world leaders at the United Nations summit in New York on the eve of the New Millennium. A decade later, it is America which has made history–even if in the opposite direction. The latest United States Census Bureau statistics show that, in 2009, one in seven Americans was living below the poverty line, the highest figure in half a century." Candidate Obama said, bring me on, I will change all of that.

After three years in power, to the chagrin of Americans, President Obama has amply demonstrated that he is capable of nothing that he said he could do. He could not quickly finish all those despicable Talibans or al Qaeda or whoever it is who hates honourable and God-fearing Ameri-

cans, he could not create a sustainable economy, could not create mean-
ingful jobs, could not ensure a proper health-care system, and he could
not control China's or Brazil's ascent (or an EU inclination to integrate
more with Russia in matters of mutual concern). Forget the big picture
of gradual ascent or integration—he could not even influence China to
revalue its currency against the dollar, or persuade "Russia, China, or
even Pakistan to follow its lead in suppressing the oil and natural gas
trade with Iran" [Dilip Hiro, *Dispatches from America*, Asia Times].
China goes from being a cheap toy and gadget manufacturer to a superpower? Brazil, a dilapidated South American mass of forest, anacondas
and piranhas, is now a major economy?? And Pakistan!! Who knows
where on the world map Pakistan is?

Do You Know Why Americans Are Angry?

The US has had a right-wing conservative worldview under both major
political parties throughout its history. As Andrew J Bacevich of the Asia
Times argues, "Both parties are war parties. They differ mainly in the
rationale they devise to argue for interventionism. The Republicans tout
liberty; the Democrats emphasise human rights. The results tend to be
the same: a penchant for activism that sustains a never-ending demand
for high levels of military outlays" [atimes.com]. That kind of right-
wing doctrine is authoritarian, traditional, hierarchical, and exclusivist in
nature.

> Traditional power relations are a guide to morality: God above man,
> man above nature, adults above children, western culture above non-
> western culture, America above other nations. (There are also bigoted
> versions: straights above gays, Christians above non-Christians, men
> above women, whites above nonwhites.) The US is seen as more moral
> than other nations and hence more deserving of power. It has the right
> to be hegemonic and must never yield its sovereignty or its overwhelm-
> ing military and economic power. It is God's own country, populated
> by the chosen people, and, surrounded by potential misbelievers and
> enemies [Hamm, *Devastating Society*, 6].

These beliefs, irrespective of who runs the state, have become the
moral imperative of Americans—the roots run extremely deep. The ascent of China goes against such beliefs. A resurgent Brazil, an economi-

cally improving India, and an un-winnable war in the Middle East; each of these clash with the core American psychology. The better-than-thou complex gets hit.

Losing the Economic Edge

Following recent world developments we are witnessing some serious reshuffling in the definition of power, for example in China. Pepe Escobar thinks that China is like Google—one cannot live without it. For any requirements, China pops up on the screen. The US in comparison is like General Motors. "With so much to offer on show, from the practical (Hyundai) to the glamorous (Aston Martin), who in his right mind wants to buy a car from GM?" China today controls 21% of all US Treasury debt, and has 25% of the world reserves. Add to that the new economic powerhouses of Brazil, South Africa, India, and Russia, and the US's flow is ebbing. Therefore, "44% of Americans, according to a recent Pew Research poll, believe that China's gross domestic product has already overtaken America's." While Wall Street initiated and executed the financial crisis of 2008, government-controlled China embarked on a journey of dominance. These days, Mr Obama asks his banks to lend (after bailing them out instead of his voters) but the "banks, as everyone knows, don't give a damn" [Pepe Escobar, *The Google-GM Summit, Asia Times*].

America today is moving from a position of independent superiority to a form of interdependent existence for the very first time. A logical person grasps the essence of it. Changes do happen, especially in this ever-changing, complex, and fluid atmosphere brought about by liquid modernity—interestingly, this is the very thing that scalds many Americans across different levels, from policy makers to voters.

Losing the Military Edge

In the new world it has become very clear that the US cannot win a war. The introductory chapter was completed in Vietnam, and the subsequent two chapters are getting written by the recent major debacles in Iraq and Afghanistan. Although most view the first war on Iraq, in 1991, as entirely successful in its (publicly) stated aims, the results are not very encouraging to the average American. The tactics of the defenders have changed and so have the battlegrounds. Trillions of dollars in military spending fails in a confrontation with ill-organised extremists and fundamentalists. The key American psychology of "Tribalism, Racism/Superiority factor and the American way of war," that has helped them many times before has come to a naught as wave after wave of defiance have not only caused red-faces in Washington but—after hitting the "sanctity" of their home ground in the recent past, have created tremendous uncertainty in the minds of morally superior Americans [Engelhardt, *In the Crosshairs*, Asia Times]. Whether this result is by chance or by choice is a debatable one, but this is irrelevant to the average American. To those reading their newspapers everyday in the US, it appears that the United States these days is having to bank on a nation like Pakistan (or Iran?) for a settlement in the Middle East to be able to bring its "boys" back home. That is like a small boil turning into herpes.

The Sum Total of Losses

> *We used to sit and talk about primal scream*
> *To exorcise our past was our adolescent dream*
> *But now it's sink or swim since your memory fails*
> *Now in Neptune's kitchen you will be food for killer whales.*
> *And on the crucifix his mother made;*
> *Hangs one more martyr to the hit parade...*
>
> —Tears for Fears, *Fish Out of Water*

People, because of their imagined righteousness, usually suffer mental pain when reality does not match their beliefs, an effect known as cognitive dissonance. Violent reactions are common. As the right wing of the US citizenry, bitter about the election of Democrat Obama, retreat into an increasingly radical right-wing shell of absolutely illogical dimensions day by day, their adherence to their ideologies exacerbates anti-Americanism even more. And that causes the Americans to retaliate further. The result? The Tea Party Movement. It comprises only about "15-20% of the electorate but has the support of half the population" [Noam Chomksy, chomsky.info]. "They cover a spectrum of extreme religious, cultural, and social beliefs with a merited reputation for weirdness and eccentricity. Virulent rightists are their heroes; right-wing think tanks and pressure groups the storm troopers. . . Among their core beliefs are the downsizing of the government, a cut in income tax, crackdown on illegal immigrants and sanctity of gun ownership" [Krishnan Srinivasan, *Time for change again*, The Telegraph (Calcutta)]. These ultra-conservatives are now the voice of a new America. They hate both Republicans and Democrats whom they think have failed to get them back their jobs, their security, and their peace of mind. They hate Barack Obama for being a Muslim, an outsider and a failure. Athough the probability of their turning into a Third Party in the 2012 elections is now non-existent, the Tea Party Movement, with unprecedented public backing, has voiced the maximum support for their choice of exclusivist Republican candidates. And who are they? From the likes of Glenn Beck, the abysmally ignorant Sarah Palin or Michelle Bachmann, to their recent favourite Newt Gingrich.

Western Europe

The results of the economic crisis in Europe are equally complicated. In Greece, Spain, Portugal, and Italy unemployed youth, workers, and lower middle-class public employees are regularly organizing general strikes, while the middle class are turning to the "hard right" and have "elected, or are on the verge of electing, reactionary prime ministers in Portugal, Spain, Greece and perhaps even in Italy." This is a practical version of what one might want to call societal polarization: a deepening rift between the institutional hard-right and the extra-parliamentary left. "In Northern and Central Europe the hard right and neo-fascist movements have made significant inroads among workers and the lower middle class at the expense of the traditional centre-left and centre-right parties. The relative stability, affluence, and stable employment of the Nordic working class has been accompanied by increasing support for racist, anti-immigrant, Islamophobic parties." [globalresearch.ca].

This is a neat orchestration: the asphyxiation of working class-based-ideology nudging the Labour and Social Democratic Parties to initiate neo-liberal programs together with the introduction of tax breaks for big business at one side; on the other side imperialist wars in Afghanistan, Iraq, Libya, and other Muslim nations while completely overlooking, and at times even catalysing, the rapid growth of neo-fascist and far-right Islamophobes by officially assaulting and villainising multiculturalism for vote-bank politics. The mainstream regimes are persistently weakening societies and promoting disharmony and extreme forms of hatred across several levels of the population.

China

A country whose humiliation by the West and Japan it has probably not forgotten, with a Grand Design for global dominance that it has never completely shared and a state-controlled 'market socialism' that has never been replicated anywhere—China is a 21st-century puzzle that the US-led West is trying to solve. Triad think-tanks are of the opinion that this is one of the supreme needs of the hour considering China's ascent to the seat of global power and its threat to the US's monopoly. Instances are everywhere, from a prolific economic boom to increasing share in oil/gas control, or from introducing a near monopoly in the manufacture of goods for the consumer market to creating the Shanghai Cooperation Organization (SCO), the only organization to counter-balance NATO in Central Asia. Western geo-strategists think that probably,

> China's grand strategy is keyed to the attainment of three interrelated objectives: first and foremost, the preservation of domestic order and well-being in the face of different forms of social strife; second, the defence against persistent external threats to national sovereignty and territory; and third, the attainment and maintenance of geopolitical influence as a major, and perhaps primary, state [Michael D Swaine, Ashley J Tellis, *Interpreting China's Grand Strategy*].

Maybe. But there is a distinct American tilt to this kind of logic and inference reminiscent of the times when the US regularly looted its Southern neighbours. There is this apprehension that growing Chinese power would increase China's level of assertion. We know that "increased level of assertion" means "aggression." Thus the expectation is that China will indulge in efforts to augment its

> military capabilities. . .develop a sphere of influence. . .acquire new or reclaim old territory. . .by penalizing, if necessary, any opponents or bystanders who resist such claims; prepare to redress past wrongs it

believes it may have suffered; attempt to rewrite the prevailing international 'rules of the game'...and, in the most extreme policy choice
imaginable, even perhaps ready itself to thwart preventive war or to
launch predatory attacks on its foes [Michael D Swaine, Ashley J Tellis, *Inerpreting China's Grand Strategy*].

Now all this is apparently legitimate in its logic. The only problem
is, China has done little of this so far and, though it has shown glimpses
of its inclination at times to do some of the above, one observes that it has
not been entirely wholehearted in its approach. The only "chessboard"
move that China has initiated so far is that of surrounding India politically and militarily from the sides of Myanmar, Pakistan, Afghanistan
and Sri Lanka. Beside this there are sporadic reports of a possible re-
inforcement of the Chinese Navy and trials to establish bases to India's
south—something that is being called "String of Pearls," including port
and airfield projects, diplomatic ties, and force modernization from the
South China Sea through the Strait of Malacca and on to the Persian
Gulf—but all currently shelved for a number of reasons [atimes.com]. If
this is to happen, to my mind a simple reason behind this act would be
perception: China sees India as America's dummy in its neighbourhood.
Now who do we blame for that?

Going back to China's "Grand Strategy:" the issue with such as-
sumptive analysis when printed and read is that it influences a lot of
people in bizarre ways. Some of them are bound to be in crucial places,
relaying the analysis to the minds of people who are critical to overall policy-making. Most of these West-influenced points-of-view make
people take defensive positions, close their minds, and manipulate racial
or civilizational points of difference in the minds of the general population. The policy makers, once they truly believe in such propaganda,
react. The result is more chaos. Then again, there may be some merit
to the arguments. As of now, no one knows, but one thing is for sure:
if chaos is the desired result, we are going the right way through such
analyses. With, or as a result of these analyses, the US has been trying
hard to get China to the table to talk. And as expected, things have not
been working out quite well on that front.

Unlike the US, China has the faculty to believe in a multi-polar world
of power sharing. Unlike the US, they can think ahead to a world expe-

riencing a "superior post-American civilization." They are eager to play a role in that. The issue is that no one from the Triad bench is inviting them keeping those points in mind. What do the Chinese think? Well, they have not been very vocal about their thoughts so far, but some really neutral and interested observers, by means of their superior reasoning, have drawn up bits and pieces. The synopsis is that China has had a continuous civilization compared to most of the Western biggies (Roman or Greek) that have collapsed and disappeared. The reason behind this, as they see it, is the Western psychology of dominance through racism or religion or commerce or war. Universalist cultures like the West or Islam, who tend to first dominate and then standardise according to their philosophy and benefit are looked down on by the Chinese intelligentsia. They think it is childish too, for only when such civilizations encounter each other, there is a war. They claim that China had found a harmonious Third Way. For their (the Chinese intelligentsia) part they argue that a "clash of civilizations" or the "end of history" can

> only occur when Universalist cultures encounter each other or prevail over each other. When two non-Universalist cultures meet, there may well be friction; but total warfare that aims at mutual annihilation is generally avoided. When, however, two Universalist cultures meet, even though they may compromise and negotiate to ensure their temporary safety, in the long run they are in principle engaged in a to-the-death struggle [Escobar, *Obama does a Globalistan*, 42–47].

Two interesting pieces of the puzzle come out of the quote: an actualization and a promise. The first one of course is the Third Way—not just lifting millions of people out of the clutches of poverty, but also promoting and encouraging non-Universalist aspirations—the only way forward in this chaos. The second one is a gentle reminder that "China would never choose the Western way, 'with their colonialist plundering of the world's resources in the process of industrialization' and would not seek superpower status like the former Soviet Union' " [Escobar, *Obama does a Globalistan*, 42–47].

The new China is showing ample signs of having traveled way ahead, rather than holding on to the ignominy of the Opium Wars, European dominance, and Japanese aggressions—an incredible achievement, especially when we consider our experience of West-hates-Islam-hates-West;

and now that they are putting across vital signs of maturity and innovation in constructive thoughts, is anybody listening?

Of course! Heads in the US, after failing to get China to the table, are already thinking of options—along the lines that they are used to. "Political economy master and professor of Sociology at Johns Hopkins University Giovanni Arrighi identifies what he calls 'three plan Bs' the U.S. had to deal with China. 1) A relentless Cold War throughout the global perimeter. 2) Accommodation—through a Kissingerian strategy of cooptation. 3) A "happy" option; the U.S. sits back, sells weapons and watches while other powers fight [Escobar, *Obama does a Globalistan*, 51]. Why reinvent the wheel?

And expectedly China, "faced with shrinking geopolitical options as the United States orchestrates a 'return to Asia,' " through small instances of surrounding India strategically, or wriggling in the Afghan equation, "is modifying its 'peaceful development' doctrine and imitating the American security-based foreign policy that has brought the world so much grief...," to the relief of American policy makers [Peter Lee, atimes.com].

Constructed Islamophobia

The great American strategist and poster-boy of US policy makers, Zbignew Brzezinski, in his book *The Grand Chessboard* outlined a strategy for America in the world. He wrote, "For America, the chief geopolitical prize is Eurasia. . .[so] how America 'manages' Eurasia is critical. Eurasia is the globe's largest continent and is geopolitically axial. A power that dominates Eurasia would control two of the world's three most advanced and economically productive regions. A mere glance at the map also suggests that control over Eurasia would almost automatically entail African subordination." Confident in his superiority as an American, he also expressed that "To put it in a terminology that harkens back to the more brutal age of ancient empires, the three grand imperatives of imperial geo-strategy are to prevent collusion and maintain security dependence among the vassals, to keep tributaries pliant and protected, and to keep the barbarians from coming together" [takeoverworld.info]. That was 1997.

Roughly during the same time, when Bill Clinton was on the throne, the neo-cons from the George Bush Senior administration formed a think tank called the Project for the New American Century, or PNAC, and published an important report called, Rebuilding America's Defenses: Strategy, Forces, and Resources for a New Century. In line with the right-wing exclusivist nature of neo-cons, the document stated that, "the United States has for decades sought to play a more permanent role in Gulf regional security. While the unresolved conflict with Iraq provides the immediate justification, the need for a substantial American force presence in the Gulf transcends the issue of the regime of Saddam Hussein" [informationclearinghouse.info].

America as an "engine of empire" with an extremely aggressive and imperialistic foreign policy has always aimed to maintain its strategic positions to secure its economic and political interests. We have a good idea of its capacities by now. Agitations in the Middle East were initially looked down upon. Brzezinski, when asked about whether he regretted "having supported the Islamic [integrisme], having given arms and advice to future terrorists, went on to emphatically record 'What is most important to the history of the world? The Taliban or the collapse of the Soviet empire? Some stirred-up Moslems or the liberation of Central Europe and the end of the cold war?' " [counterpunch.org]. Islamic reactions were nothing more than "some stirred up Moslems," in other words minor hurdles.

The 9/11 attacks among other things shattered the "stirred up Moslems" picture, and brought forth a bigger and more intimidating idea of Islamic terrorism. Capitalization was instant too. From the war in Iraq, to bombing Afghanistan, to extraterritorial incarceration of hundreds of suspects at Guantanamo Bay, the Bush Gang started pursuing their 'democratization' agenda vigorously. Back home, pacts were made with the people. Repression, the moment any one challenged the status quo, was initiated. The rest of the population could "enjoy freedom to travel, to live more or less as they wished to and to make and spend their money" [Kampfner, *Freedom for Sale*, 5]. The commoners never challenged and the wealthier ones were duly protected against the use of "arbitrary state power," and the government invented the right to arrest, detain (and torture) and deport any foreigner it liked, through the Patriot Act. Surveillance was increased to a greater degree than the world had ever witnessed (refer to the Lockheed Martin observation in "Of Globalisation"). Some cities, like London, now have a camera fixed almost everywhere watching its people. During the time of Blair the Parliament passed "forty-five criminal justice laws. . ., creating more than three thousand new criminal offences. Police and security forces were given greater powers of arrest and detention; all institutions of state were granted increased rights to snoop; individuals were required to hand over unprecedented data" [Kampfner, *Freedom for Sale*, 197].

Islamophobia, a clear case of a mutant creation at one time, presented opportunistic advantages to the greed-system. The cause-effect cycle is an interesting one. More repression and hegemonic ambitions resulted in larger proportions of Islamic reaction, that in turn was positioned to aggravate fear in people's minds, and that helped the military-industrial establishment to beef up the security business and to bring more pressure on Islam and the Middle East. At the start of the twenty-first century, the US has nothing more to offer the world other than tanks, planes, ammunition, and surveillance systems. This is not a good position to be in—all the more reason why security had to be subsidised into a lucrative business model for as long as possible, at the cost of millions of lives.

* * * * *

Each product has its own life cycle. Fear of Communism, once constructed and released into the market, lived for some time. Eventually it got scrapped. At 2012, although Islamophobia has some way to go, it is staring at a rather dull future and threatening to become a has-been very soon. Al Qaeda, albeit modernised and decentralised, clearly lacks the wherewithal to continue its war against the West. They are on life-support these days—popping up wherever Uncle Sam needs a cook-up, and disappearing from the headlines during the rest of the year. The few other "terrorist/fundamentalist" entities or nations are busy within their own world too: the Taliban are more interested in dismembering their men, stoning or mutilating their women, and basically minding their own business. The other "radicals" like Hezbollah or Hamas are more concentrated on their efforts to effect developments in their respective nations, or in wresting more rights from Israel. Iran, one of the "axis of evil," is more keen on its civilian programmes, strategizing for a greater share in the affairs of the Middle East, and consolidating commercial relations with the world wherever possible. But a puppet breaking strings is not desirable, so all of them are on prop-stilts, being prodded regularly to dance whenever required, because it is still too early to phase out Islamophobia. The fittest example is the current series of conflicts raging in the Arab world, dubbed as Arab Spring. Characteristic Western interference may well witness a series of fresh recruits under the different Islamic extremist banners in the near future.

Then there are volunteers as well. They make this equation complex. Saudi Arabia and Pakistan, the lifetime buddies of the US, keep promoting extreme hatred among the ignorant masses of Wahhabi/Deobandi Muslims against anything that is deemed un-Islamic—probably to create that breathing space for America and the greed-system to reorganise and re-embark on the next hate cycle (and even though Pakistan these days keeps oscillating across uncertainties in relations with the US, the Islamic hardcore teachings and their effects have taken their own course). There would be takers too, considering the perpetual poverty and illiteracy among a large section of Islam's population.

On the other hand, it is a damning situation for these two nations, particularly Pakistan. Saudi oil reserves have peaked. The monarchy is really obsolete. The government has no tax-mechanism for its citizens, which is only one way out of many of telling its people that since they do not pay tax they should not expect any reforms or developments. But that is still manageable, because once reforms are introduced (if and when) they could possibly bring about some positive changes in the peninsula. For Pakistan, a state that has grown up consuming a staple of obsessive hatred towards India, fostering terrorism probably had its own benefits at one point; but as a result, it looks like a nearly impossible journey to global standardization now. Islamic fundamentalism, extreme intolerance, and terror campaigns have now become a kind of virus that is gradually rendering the entire socio-political structure useless. The only solace is the unwavering US support in all matters, even when it came to harbouring and nurturing terrorists. And until about the beginning of 2011 Pakistan was doing a damn good balancing act, possibly to enhance the US's toe-hold in central Asia. But after a series of spats between these two long-time buddies and the subsequent violation of its territorial sovereignty by the Big Brother, the relationship apparently has hit rock bottom. But terrorism has not dissipated, and it finally looks exactly like what the wise (and even the not-so-wise) men predicted long ago: the extremist elements have gone on auto-pilot. They are a subterranean entity of their own who do not need establishment support to sustain themselves anymore. Debatable or not, Pakistan is disintegrated and in serious trouble, and if a series of short-term fixes through the decades is what they thought would eventually liberate them and establish their Golden Age in the post-modern world—they are being incredibly daft.

Back within the scope of the New World Order, once the US is ready for the next battle again, the shape of things to come would then be defined by its animosity with China (and to a lesser extent, Iran) in their quest for central Asian energy resources. America, to my mind, is getting ready. Though China has given some indication that it does not aspire to play by the rules of Washington, America knows of no other games, save the ones that have Cold War written all over them. In its endeavour to drag Iran and China into a stage they do not seem interested to share, the US has them surrounded from nearly all angles with military bases and is trying to restrict or has already restricted their trade relations. Even though the second nuisance does not matter much, especially for China, because the world today cannot do without their exports, it is the military presence that might prompt them to get into an arms race, or a self-destructive race of some kind—something that the US dearly wants.

From direct interventions as in Iraq or Afghanistan, Washington has subtly moved to "outsourcing" intervention. The use of Britain and France in Libya and a trend to possibly involve Turkey in Syria—the outcome of these might provide pointers to rewriting the rules of engagement. "Outsourcing" as a business strategy has proven its cost efficacy many times before, and in cases relating to international conflicts it keeps the popular-opinion graph intact. It may not promise an immediate change in regime, but it can certainly promise a destabilizing effect. And while destabilization was not at all an option in the case of Libya, it will do fine in the case of Iran or China.

I maintain that reactions, by nature, are mostly dicey, but the facts are that (1) China is gradually getting sucked into a game that it did not intend to play, and (2) the future of the New World Order will largely be determined by China's response.

9 After Greed — *We, the People*

The line it is drawn, the curse it is cast
The slow one now, will later be fast
As the present now will later be past
The order is rapidly fadin'
And the first one now, will later be last
For the times they are a-changin'.

—Bob Dylan, *The Times They Are A-Changin'*

In order to highlight a few key results of the Greed System's predominance in human thoughts and actions, this book spread its observations across a fair portion of the globe to provide illustrations. There are innumerable other instances I have left out; one major example is the poor fate of nearly the entire continent of Africa. There are two reasons for these omissions. The first is that I did not intend to write a really fat book that might deter young people from picking up and reading it. It is critically important that the next generation understands the pattern, and they do have an inclination towards reading materials that are less bulky. Second, this will give me a chance to reiterate the operative rationale used in this book to point out something brand new to readers in some future work.

Let us sum up what we have covered so far and take a look at the patterns that emerge. Europe's domination of the greed system lasted for two hundred years. It was brought down by two large wars. The greed system was Americanised soon afterwards and its triumph over the rest of the world reached new heights in little time. It was bolstered uniquely through Communism first, and when that faltered through constructed Islamophobia. Communism was potent enough to survive the US onslaught for close to seventy years. Will Islamophobia manage to also? The signs say maybe not. It is fading after around thirty years of service and utility as a product to catalyze the wealth-accumulation mechanism. Eventually it will be squashed through a probable Balkanization of Pakistan and Afghanistan. Then terrorism like Communism will be a thing of the past and will hardly register a blip on the global radar after, say, a hundred years.

Will the US's (and the Triad's) greed-based supremacy continue unabated for two hundred years? Well, efforts are on to ensure that, and there are serious endeavours to construct China as the new façade after the fall of terrorism as the ruling Fear Factor. There is already an orchestration of initiating annoyance in the domestic American circuit relating to China's ascent, thanks to the media's ability to "manufacture consent.". And there is nothing more desirable than wholehearted domestic support for a covert or overt aggression against China—following the lessons learnt from the past. It lends legitimacy, washes away guilt, brings in votes, but most of all, helps grow business.

There were chances, some really good ones, to alter this model. The best one that comes to mind was when Barack Nobel-Peace Obama came to power. He could have, as mentioned before, bailed out his domestic population first, following the recession. Half the world was actually expecting him to do just that. He could have recognised that it was America and its habit of bolstering Sunni militancy that was behind the cause of all the problems in central Asia— from the Middle East to Chechnya to Kashmir. He could have effected new measures to check the unbridled glut of global hypercapitalism. These would have made history, both conceptually and practically. But Obama proved to all of us that he was only about rhetoric—he was just another politician, a hollow individual driven by the Washington policymaker-corporate nexus; an also-ran.

New World Paradoxes

At the start of the twenty-first century we encounter a few unique phenomena. Primary among them is the exploitation of human lives as liquid capital. Some are made weapons while some are made targets, some are made to starve while some are made to labour—all of these are done to justify some bizarre point or other. Someone makes killing a business, someone makes defending human rights a racket. The less-unfortunates that live in more or less free societies are kept constantly under fear. This perennial fear for so many things, recognised or not, has triggered two unique patterns. People in relatively advanced societies regularly sell their civil rights and liberty to purchase some security. Unaware of the cause-effect cycle, they wholeheartedly endorse their candidate through what is usually known as democracy in the developed world, and then hand over their liberty to their leaders and keep themselves out of matters of state, thinking they are safe. People who are relatively regressive in matters pertaining to constructive intelligence respond to fear in a different way. They turn backwards and try to take solace from their religion, developing and displaying extreme strains of religious intolerance, often bordering on hate-culture and physical violence. These two broad types remain in a state of perpetual friction with each other: with each passing day the gap between them widens. Both think they are justified, both think that is the only way to be secure.

Unfortunately neither set realises that the chaos is orchestrated.

Democracy in itself has become severely mutated, making things a whole lot easier for the political leaders. A government of today derives legitimacy not from delivering quantifiable growth and developments, but simply from having been voted in. Therefore, "the legitimacy of democracy in many ways" absolves governments "from the necessity of performing." Democracy today has been carefully devised to become a "vehicle to deliver consumption" in an era of globalised wealth. Geo-economics and geo-politics have been married off for some time now. The results are visible. "Economic growth, rather than being a force for democratic involvement, [has] reinforced the confidence of business and political elites. They [have] thrived because they [have] reinterpreted the basic tenets of democracy to suit their needs; all linked to greed for more" [Kampfner, *Freedom for Sale*, 151, 262].

Everything is on credit these days, from consumer durables to nationalism, and people seem to have more or less accepted credit societies. We idolise consumerism, have renounced the idea of savings, and have become more or less indifferent to the idea of larger conflicts or the discerning role of a government in the fate of their nations. Nationalism is passé, save those rare cases of a football or cricket tournament or terrorist attacks. Our lives have become increasingly constricted, often limited to the spread of our towns or cities or religions; for some, it hardly travels beyond their friends' circle. Our "enemies are unknown, wars are unde-clared," all within narrowed versions of our space. The only surviving "logic is fear." And when events like 9/11 or the 2008 recession occur, we are shocked to discover how thin and fragile a cushion we have to fall back on [preterhuman.net].

After Greed

The only thing that would redeem mankind is cooperation.
    —Bertrand Russell

This planet is a single unit. But it appears that, to the multitude of a global population lost in their personal strifes this fact is not pertinent enough. And though no one looks in a mood to register or agree with this observation, an incredible number of people are relentlessly think-ing about how to make this world a better place. Michel Chossudovsky, Noam Chomsky, William Blum, Amartya Sen, Pepe Escobar, and a lot of other people not mentioned in this book are untiringly pushing against the huge mass of the greed system with immense intellectual resources, waiting for newer generations to at least recognise the drift and chip-in with some physical presence. Far removed from the world of conflicts and politics, here is a concept that can possibly augur a vision of a society beyond the reaches of the current greed-system. I am not an economist, or a social scientist, I do not have political backers or ideological affil-iations; I do not subscribe to conventional logic. But disagreeing with the mainstream has its advantages. One is this: I can put forth any idea that looks beneficial to this world, to its plant and animal kind , with-out having to overthink its effect on the fate of the transnational-political brotherhood.

In his forthcoming book Cooperative Capitalism, political economist and author Dr J.W. Smith puts across a thesis that cuts through the monopoly and property-rights structure that he considers as the base be-hind much of the modern world's misery. Pointing out the basic cunning in the world-dominating greed-based capitalist system, he argues that "your property rights laws today, as applied to nature's resources and technologies, is nothing more than aristocracy's property rights law, ex-clusive title to nature's wealth which she offers to all for free.". Think about it for a while. After reading this, does logic not say that natural resources in a particular geography and its indigenous populations, not the capitalists, should establish the use-value of land? [Smith, *Co-operative Capitalism*, 271–281]. But historically, from plundering the Native Americans or massacring the Indian subcontinent and shipping off the wealth to England, to a more recent robbing of half of the Middle East through control of energy resources, has that ever happened? Factually, over the centuries, to protect and increase their wealth and power, the greedsters have done whatever was required, from tweaking the principle of monopolization of lands to banks, patents, communications, insurance or healthcare—anything that you can think of.

The brilliance of Dr Smith's thesis is that if such a system were achieved the "rental values" of such resources used by local populations (populations equates to customers, consumers, entrepreneurs, and producers here) "can provide the funding of essential social services" like roads, railways, sewers, electricity, education, health systems, or retirements, even as all taxes disappear. Which means from consumers to producers, and even those governing—all pay those rental values. Naturally the concept of "tax" gets redundant in the process, and all enjoy, on average, a higher standard of living. Of course, "We are not talking about personal property, which was build by labor, properly exclusively owned, and retaining, or collecting, rental values is proper. We are talking about the wealth of nature, which was not produced by labour and belongs to everybody" [Smith, *Co-operative Capitalism*, 271–281].

Visualise a society that has been created by those who work the soil and in industries. They and (if all jobs are shared equally) everybody, are the rightful owners. Resource and land rents are collected from homeowners as well as corporations, industries, etc. that utilise that land and the natural resources on and under it to produce and distribute both consumer products and social services. The funds collected, plus the profits of socially-owned banks, are easily balanced to fund all infrastructure, all essential social services, and all governments. The cost of some social services will drop by half or more and governments will operate at a fraction of current costs. Factually, once each region, each state, each county, each community, and each individual has full and equal rights, governments would only meet occasionally. With everyone knowing both their rights and others' rights. Corruption and other roadblocks to efficiency simply disappear. After all, every citizen will be able to look at any aspect of this economy and judge its efficiency.

> This requires sharing the 'productive' remaining jobs, equal pay for equally-productive labour, and, where applicable, equal right to created and saved finance capital. In a nutshell this scenario eliminates both unproductive labour and unproductive finance capital, reroutes the flow of money towards the producers of our wealth and services, and ensures both social health and a quality life for all, even as it encourages entrepreneurial aspirations. Incredible in its simplicity, powerful in its appeal, this simple social structure that all citizens can visualise could very well be a balanced alternative for today's greed system or 'theft-capitalism' and a catalyst for a peaceful planet [Smith, *Co-operative Capitalism*, 271–281].

> If Iceland, all Eastern Europe, Greece, Ireland, Portugal, Italy, and Spain pay the rental values of nature's resources and technologies— and their bank profits—to themselves (redirecting the flow of money), as opposed paying to bond holders, that would fund their economy and give them both the time and money to restructure their industries to compete efficiently across the world [Smith, *Co-operative Capitalism*, 203].

Has this been tried out ever before? You bet! David Schweickart tells us China's banks were socially owned, and under a policy of the people owning the land but society collecting the rent, between 1979 and 1984 (just about 4 years!), the number of rural Chinese living in poverty declined from more than 200 million to 70 million. That being said, it is also true that all of this is not going to be easy. If control of oil or gas or strategic points along land or sea routes can give rise to so much friction, to think that the Big Brothers would easily give-in to those people or the school of thought trying to disrupt something as cardinal as the greed system, is naïveté. When the developed world's economies collapse and the imperialists realise that their fallacy has destroyed their nice little racket, they will instinctively want to activate their mighty military or their covert intelligence and operations systems. Now you know why the US is hell-bent on playing another Cold War with China. Thankfully the Vietnam, Afghanistan, and Iraq fiascos have proved that winning even apparently easy wars is not so easy anymore.

Evolution has never been a cakewalk. The reason behind trying to chart this line of thought was to bring some points onto the table. They have been brought on. You would have already realised the incredible presence, reach, and influence of greed across all levels—religion, politics, economics, or society—through the earlier chapters. Now you also have a fair idea of things to come and/or changes that can be brought about. The underlying differentiator is intent. As far as perception management of the media is concerned, a whole lot of it has been thoroughly shaken since the last decade of the last century. With the internet and mobility, information is freely available. Personally, even about ten years ago, I could never have dreamt of such ease of access to so many different authors' and thinkers' works as I have had in the last five years. At the level of one-on-one and small group interactions that capability is gradually getting to be a huge differentiator, as it is slowly heralding the beginning of an off-season for thought monopolization.

The future depends on what we want, how we want it. We could choose a continuation of this disdainful run of the greed system that chews up and pollutes everything within sight—that is fast making this world unlivable for future generations—or we could wake up the vanishing thinking class and decide to educate people about it.

> "Who knows, perhaps the children will thank us if we at least try to stop the greed-mongering; start doing the right thing; stop doing what is patently unsustainable and start moving in a new direction toward sustainable lifestyles and right-sizing "too big to fail" corporate leviathans before the world is ruined [Steve Salmony, *Deluded, Greedy and Obese*, informationclearinghouse.info].

We speak best when we speak for our world—the need of the hour is a uniformity in the comprehension of the dimension of "Our World."

Postscript

With enemies like these, who needs friends?

  —Pepe Escobar

Osama bin Laden finally lay dead, dumped somewhere in the waters of the Arabian Sea. This product of US Cold-War foreign policy was befriended, manipulated, nurtured, cultured, ostracised, and later destroyed. When America needed to give the Soviets "their Vietnam" in Afghanistan, Mujaheedins like Osama allied to their cause. He was even Americanised to "Tim Osman" by the CIA during those days. When Bush needed a push towards securing his second term, Osama lent credibility through 9/11. No concrete investigations could conclusively pin the blame on him, but Bush screamed his lungs out and gullible people believed. (Why are people invariably so gullible by the way?). When the military-industrial complex needed a shot in the arm, al Qaeda blasted throughout Europe and Asia and did the needful. When the US needed bunkers in Afghanistan to monitor the nuclear states of Pakistan, Iran, China, and India, or look out for escape routes of Turkmen gas to free markets, Osama supposedly hid there to prompt them to organise a massive manhunt that went along for eleven long years, transforming Afghanistan into a central Asian satellite of the US. Finally, at the end of a disastrous domestic recovery programme, when the Obama-led Greed System needed yet another term in the White House, Osama got hunted down, shot in the face, and dumped in the sea. All in good time.

  While Obama argued on national TV immediately after the hunt that the US delivered "justice," a number of geopolitical experts opined that it was more "revenge." A pertinent point being that justice required an obligatory court, a judge, and in some cases a jury. It required crime-scene investigation, conclusive evidences, lawyers, and courtroom contests too.

  Justice or revenge? In fact it is neither. The removal of Osama is akin to, and as basic as, the removal of a pawn from the chessboard. So your pawn has outlived its physical usefulness and needs to be utilised in its death. What would you do? Prepare an emotional farewell speech and a retirement package? Hardly. As Jeffrey Archer says, "don't get mean, get even;" the extreme emotions that demand justice or resort to revenge do not apply here. With Barrack Obama's second term looming, and his incapable governance resulting in a dwindling popular base, it was time to utilise Osama the pawn's physical form one last time.

While it lasted, this was indeed an outstanding wedding. And now the ghost of Osama the pawn promises to look after the spouse's well-being unwaveringly. "Till death do us part" does not apply here. With the 2011 series of revolutions rocking Tunisia, Egypt, Syria, Yemen, and Bahrain, with a key fraction of the Muslim world genuinely trying to steer towards a more Westernised form of state governance, al Qaeda was threateningly sidelined from the beginning of 2011. Salafi-Jihadi volatility, Sunni militancy, brand Osama, terror campaigns, etc—one of the most important verticals supporting the existence of the United States Military Industrial Complex was staring at a shaky yearly forecast. Not anymore, to the relief of the Fat-cats; this death promises to bring billion-dollar deals onto the table. The military-industrial propagandists can sit back, enjoy their cognacs, and reap their profit as the world promises to gear up for another surge of Islamic militancy, far removed from the logical assertion towards self determination recently witnessed in Tahrir Square—with a little help from their "friends."

To the world the US-led NATO forces fight a "war on terror" against the likes of al-Qaeda or the Taliban. To the inner-circle comprised of the politicians and the policy makers it is an entirely different equation. No allegiance is permanent enough, no enemy is enemy enough, and the only wars that are fought are the ones that are profitable. The signs are everywhere.

The Tahrir Square initiative has been systematically whitewashed. Egypt did manage to throw Hosni Mubaarak out but these days the self determination mantra is barely audible. The country is being ruled by a military regime—no change in governing policies. The Syrian uprising is threatened to be "adopted" by NATO. If this hijack happens, the result will be the same, to the horror of the Syrians. No one gives a damn. Bahrain's uprising has been violently suppressed. Because of the foundations of the uprising, almost all its people are opposed to the US and its Middle-East policies. The Libyan rebels that removed Qaddafi from the hot-seat, while enjoying overt support from NATO, also dipped their hands into the al-Qaeda bag for some covert assistance—something that Qaddafi kept on stressing on television, and was customarily ignored—as the "madman" that he was widely considered, thanks to mainstream media. There were no repercussions, and the facts were suppressed. [telegraph.co.uk]

NATO had to do it. After all, al-Qaeda (read: Constructed Islamic Fundamentalism) is the alter-ego of the Military Industrial Complex.

Remember writer-activist William Blum? That gentleman has been completely sidelined by the American mainstream media. He said that whenever any state among the so-called Third World initiated an attempt towards self-determination, or displayed a tendency to pursue a path of development independent of United States, the state was pushed back to medieval times by Big Brother. So, it's goodbye popular revolutions and welcome remixed extremism. Osama the pawn, alive and dead, continues to serve his creator—the Greed System.

As the 2012 election approaches the Republicans and the Democrats gear up to flog the new bogey-man: China. Evidently that is not going to solve the economic stagnation that the US faces; aggressive foreign policies focused on intimidating and bullying other nations are good as long as the economy is good—not the other way round. But the huge propaganda machine will yet again make sure that American voters buy the new carrot. Republicans or Democrats, whoever closes the sale effectively gets the Presidential palace and the chair—but like Osama bin Laden the White House too will continue to serve the Greed System.

The Devil doesn't sweat the details.

Bibliography

Bauman, Zygmunt. *Liquid Modernity.* Australia: Polity Press, 2000.

Blum, William. *Killing Hope.* Monroe, ME: Common Courage Press, 2008. Print.

—. *Rogue State: A Guide to the World's Only Superpower.* Monroe, Me: Common Courage Press, 2005.

Brzezinski, Zbigniew. *The Grand Chessboard: American Primacy And Its Geostrategic Imperatives.* New York: Basic Books, 1997.

Burke, Jason. *Al-Qaeda: The True Story of Radical Islam.* New York: I.B. Tauris & Co., 2003.

Chomsky, Noam. David Barsamian and Hamish Hamilton, interviewers. *Imperial Ambitions—Conversations On the Post 9/11 World.* New York: Metropolitan Books, 2005.

—. *Turning the Tide: U.S. Intervention in Central America and the Struggle for Peace.* New York: South End Press, 1999.

—. *Year 501—The Conquest Continues.* Cambridge, MA: South End Press, 1993.

Chossudovsky, Michel. *America's War on Terrorism.* Quebec: Global Research, 2005.

—. *Globalisation of Poverty and the New World Order, The,* 2nd ed. Quebec: Global Research, 2003.

Escobar, Pepe. *Globalistan: How the Globalized World is Dissolving Into Liquid War.* Ann Arbor, MI: Nimble Books, 2006.

—. *Obama does Globalistan.* Ann Arbor, MI: Nimble Books, 2009.

Hamm, Bernd. *Devastating Society: The Neo-Conservative Assault on Democracy and Justice.* London: Pluto Press, 2005.

Hussain, Zahid. *Frontline Pakistan: The Struggle with Militant Islam.* New York: Columbia UP, 2007.

Kampfner, John. *Freedom for Sale: How We Made Money and Lost Our Liberty.* London: Simon & Schuster, 2009., by John Kampfner,

Simon and Schuster

Kennedy, David, and Thomas Bailey. *American Spirit, The, vol. 1.* Boston: Wadsworth, 2006.

Leffler, Melvyn P. *A Preponderance of Power: National Security, the Truman Administration, and the Cold War.* Stanford: Stanford UP, 1993.

Milton-Edwards, Beverly. *Islamic Fundamentalism since 1945.* New York: Routledge, 2005.

Nehru, Jawaharlal. *The Discovery of India.* Centenary Edition. Oxford: Oxford UP, 1994, by Jawaharlal Nehru

Perkins, John. *Confessions of an Economic Hit Man.* New York: Penguin, 2004.

Prouty, Fletcher. *JFK: The CIA, Vietnam, and the Plot to Assassinate John F. Kennedy, 2d ed.* New York: Kensington, 2003.

Rashid, Ahmed. *Descent into Chaos: The United States and the Failure of Nation Building in Pakistan, Afghanistan, and Central Asia.* New York: Penguin, 2008.

Saad-Ghorayeb, Amal. *Hizbu'llah: Politics & Religion.* London: Pluto Press, 2002.

Smith, J.W. *Cooperative Capitalism.* Appomattox, VA: Institute for Economic Democracy Press (forthcoming).

Swaine, Michael, and Ashley J. Tellis. *Interpreting China's Grand Strategy: Past, Present, and Future.* Washington D.C.: RAND, 2000.

Weeks, John. "Globalize, Globa-lize, Global Lies: Myths of the World Economy in the 1990's." *Phases of Capitalist Development.* Robert Albritton, Makoto Itoh, Richard Westra, and Alan Zuege, eds. New York, Palgrave, 2001.

Yergin, Daniel. *The Prize: The Epic Quest for Oil, Money & Power.* New York: Simon & Schuster, 1991.

Zepezauer, Mark. *The CIA's Greatest Hits.* Tuscon: Odonian Press, 2002.

Frequently used Websites

americaversuseurope.com
atimes.com
chomsky.info
counterpunch.org
countrystudies.us
ezinearticles.com
globaled.org
globalresearch.ca
halexandria.org
harvardwarcriminals.blogspot.com
ied.info
informationclearinghouse.info
internationalpeaceandconflict.org
killinghope.org
lngworldnews.com
mrzine.monthlyreview.org
takeoverworld.info
thirdworldtraveller.com
tomdispatch.com
zompist.com

Index

www.ingramcontent.com/pod-product-compliance
Lightning Source LLC
Chambersburg PA
CBHW031510270326
41930CB00006B/342